Inpatient
Group
Psychotherapy

A PSYCHODYNAMIC PERSPECTIVE

INPATIENT GROUP PSYCHOTHERAPY

A Psychodynamic Perspective

Cecil A. Rice, Ph.D.
Director, Postgraduate Training Center
Boston Institute for Psychotherapies
Boston, Massachusetts

J. Scott Rutan, Ph.D.
Assistant Clinical Professor of Psychology,
Department of Psychiatry
Harvard Medical School
Boston, Massachusetts

Director, Center for Group Therapy
Massachusetts General Hospital
Boston, Massachusetts

Macmillan Publishing Company
NEW YORK

Collier Macmillan Canada, Inc.
TORONTO

Collier Macmillan Publishers
LONDON

Macmillan Publishing Company
866 Third Avenue, New York 10022

Collier Macmillan Canada, Inc.
Collier Macmillan Publishers • London

Library of Congress Cataloging-in-Publication Data

Rice, Cecil A.
  Inpatient group psychotherapy.

  Includes bibliographies and index.
  1. Group psychotherapy.   2. Psychiatric hospital
patients.   I. Rutan, J. Scott.   II. Title.   [DNLM:
1. Inpatients—psychology.   2. Interpersonal Relations.
3. Psychotherapy, Groups—methods. WM 430 R495i]
RC488.R53   1987   616.89′152   86-31243
ISBN 0-02-399730-3

Printing: 1 2 3 4 5 6 7 8   Year: 7 8 9 0 1 2 3 4 5

DEDICATION

TO
SHIRLEY AND CATHY
JANE, GREGORY, AND CHRISTOPHER

PREFACE

We decided to write this book out of our conviction that the pathologies that confront today's psychiatric patients are predominately interpersonal. Although there are intrapsychic, biological, sociological, and other sources of psychological distress, the patients we see tend to experience their discomfort primarily with regard to their capacity to gain what they desire or need from their relationships. With that in mind, group therapy is a particularly vital and powerful therapeutic response. Furthermore, we are convinced that we exist in an era when there is an alarming trend toward understanding individual patients as collections of symptoms, rather than as whole people. Today one "has a depression" rather than "is depressed."

In psychiatric hospitals patients are often just contained, calmed down, and their symptoms are lessened or removed with little concern for what role or meaning the symptoms may have had.

In other words, the psychodynamic understanding of psychological illness is losing ground in favor of newer, presumably quicker and more cost efficient treatments. In the process we feel patients are often misunderstood and mistreated, and the richness and complexity of human experience are minimized.

We present an approach to inpatient group therapy that allows clinicians to treat their patients as more than just symptoms. Rather, it is our hope that clinicians will see their patients' symptoms as communications about themselves, about the nature of their inner lives and their personal relations.

Inpatient groups do not exist in isolation. They are profoundly affected, as are their members, by the context in which they are set, by the nature of staff relations, by the patients who are in them, and by the numerous other events that take place in a hospital.

It is that complexity, richness, chaos, and order of inpatient psychotherapy groups that we are addressing in this book. We will focus primarily on groups in acute care hospitals where the average patient stay is 21 days. We do *not* discuss activities groups and special interest groups, important as those groups are in an inpatient setting. Rather we have chosen to limit ourselves to those groups with which we are most familiar. It is our expectation, however, that some of the dynamics of the psychotherapy groups we discuss will be applicable in a number of ways to the other groups.

In Chapter 1 we begin with an overview of the history of inpatient groups and their relationship to the major cultural changes of the last two hundred years. In Chapter 2 we outline the major psychodynamic concepts on which this book is based. Included is a section on systems theory that helps to bridge the gap between the heavy individual and interpersonal emphasis of psychodynamic theory and the more complex dynamics of the group and the hospital. In Chapters 3 and 4 we discuss the dynamics of inpatient groups and hospitals, respectively.

Chapter 5 describes how an inpatient group therapy program may be established. Its suggestions are based on the thesis that for an inpatient group to work effectively it must be thoroughly integrated, both philosophically and practically, into the hospital's treatment program. It must be a primary treatment mode within the hospital's overall treatment plan.

The techniques of leading a group are the focus of Chapter 6. We consider sophisticated listening by therapists to be the essential technique in leading a psychodynamic inpatient group. Accurate, empathic listening determines how, when, and what interventions psychodynamic therapists make. In Chapter 7 we take the role of listening a step farther as we address the demands of some of the difficult patients and groups an inpatient therapist frequently faces.

Finally, in Chapter 8 we address the role, dynamics, and leadership of the community meeting. We consider the community meeting to be the central group of the hospital. It provides much of the glue that holds the hospital community together and has direct import, for good and ill, on all the other treatment modalities, including group therapy. When this meeting is ineffective, all other treatments are adversely affected; conversely, when this meeting is effective, all other treatments benefit.

We cannot go farther without expressing our heartfelt thanks and deepest appreciation to the many individuals who provided invaluable assistance to us in the writing of this book. In some cases, as with Shirley and Jane, our wives, or Cathy, Gregory, and Christopher, our children, that help came in the form of infinite support and love. Their compassion, and their willingness to be without us when our writing took us from them, sustained us. In other cases the assistance came from dear friends and colleagues who pored laboriously over the text and provided corrections, suggestions, congratulations, and directions that were of inestimable value. In all cases their assistance was a labor of love, because all they will receive is this mention, a free copy of the book, and our undying gratitude. Meanwhile, their efforts, ideas and scholarship appear on every page. At the risk of unfortunately omitting some names, we nonetheless want to cite in particular Drs. Thomas Aiello, Anne Alonso, Raymond Battegay, Howard Kibel, Doris Manzer-Benaron, Stanley Roskind, Walt Stone, and Ms. Irene Rutchick. Each of these individuals is an important scholar in inpatient group therapy and a friend, whose generous willingness to give freely of time and expertise has improved this text. Lastly, for her editorial assistance, encouragement and support, we wish to express our appreciation to Ms. Sarah Boardman.

Cecil A. Rice, Ph.D.
J. Scott Rutan, Ph.D.

CONTENTS

Inpatient
Group
Psychotherapy

A PSYCHODYNAMIC PERSPECTIVE

1

History of Inpatient Group Psychotherapy

Reports of kindly, let alone therapeutic, treatment of the mad are limited in the history of Western civilization. Incarceration of some sort seems to have been the most common pattern, whether it was at sea aboard narrenschiffen *(ships for the mad), within the towers of the town walls, or in special institutions. . . .*[1]

HISTORY OF INPATIENT PSYCHIATRIC CARE

It is very difficult to chronicle the institutional treatment of mental illness because insanity has been understood so differently throughout history. The aberrant of society have been held with wild ambivalence. They have been esteemed as prophets and killed as witches. They have been sources of terror, awe, and bewilderment. Society's responses to them have been as varied as its understanding of them. Depending on the era and age, the mentally ill were considered possessed by demons to be shunned or children of God to be followed, the worst and best of society.

Hippocrates (c. 460–355 B.C.) viewed mental illness as an understandable, medical phenomenon. His early hypotheses included attributing insanity to increased humidity in the brain, understanding depression as an excess of black bile, and tracing hysteria to the womb moving about within a woman's body. Although the specific suggestions are humorous by modern standards, it is clear that Hippocrates did not view mental illness as "evil" or deserving of punishment. His stance was not always the predominant one.

Earlier civilizations (e.g., the Sumerians, 200 B.C.) often attributed

1

the unusual behaviors of the mentally ill to possession by evil spirits. This led naturally to dramatic societal responses. Often the "possessed" individuals were beaten, exiled, or even killed. Because the understanding of the behaviors was religious, the "treaters" were usually religious figures. In some cases there was an attempt at "healing" the possessed individual, and this typically involved some magical powers of the healer. In American history, the mentally ill were often deemed sinners, possessed by Satan. A great many were doubtless judged to be witches and killed.

The past two hundred years have seen the rise, and in one instance the fall, of three major humane movements for the treatment of hospitalized mental patients. They are the Moral Treatment, the Milieux Therapy, and the Therapeutic Community movements. A psychodynamic thread runs through the latter two movements.

MORAL TREATMENT

The moral treatment movement began in the late eighteenth century and continued into the middle of the nineteenth century. It began during a period of social reform in France. Philippe Pinel (1745–1826) is usually viewed as the founder of the movement. As head of the Bicetre, a mental hospital in Paris, Pinel began a treatment program that provided compassion and understanding on an individual basis. Through Pinel's efforts, hospitals for the insane began paying attention to the comfort and safety of their patients. At the same time, William Tuke, a Quaker in York, England, established *The Retreat,* another famous humane treatment program. Not long after this, Benjamin Rush established the first psychiatric department in America, at Pennsylvania Hospital in Philadelphia.

In short order, other hospitals founded on these humane principles began appearing: Friends' Asylum in Philadelphia, Pennsylvania, McLean Hospital in Boston, Massachusetts, Hartford Retreat in Hartford, Connecticut, Butler Hospital in Providence, Rhode Island, and Worcester State Hospital in Worcester, Massachusetts.[2]

This reform movement was truly international in scope, and although moral treatment was never fully defined, it did carry particular meanings for those who practiced it. Bockoven noted that "the early psychiatrist used 'moral' as the equivalent of 'emotional' or 'psychological' . . . It meant compassionate and understanding treatment of innocent sufferers.''[3] Actual practice varied from hospital to hospital, but moral treatment usually included kindly care, fresh air, and social interaction among patients and staff.[4] Also, patients often carried out some responsible tasks.

Advocates of moral treatment claimed a cure rate as high as 95 to 100 percent. Although those reports were most likely highly inflated, it seems true that when individuals were placed in these humane treatment facilities early in the course of their illness, they usually did well.

Unfortunately, the moral treatment movement became a victim of its own success. In the mid-1800s, for instance, Dorothea Dix,[5] impressed with the efforts of the professionals in these facilities, became a very effective voice in advocating the building of large hospitals and enlarging current ones to provide moral treatment. Ironically, as larger and larger facilities were built, patients ultimately became isolated and abandoned. By the mid-1800s, psychiatric hospitals often were no longer bastions of humane treatment but had become large custodial facilities where intense individualized contact was impossible. The basic care that Dorothea Dix hoped for never materialized. This was particularly true of the large state hospitals, where the very success of the earlier psychiatric hospitals had led to a flooding of these facilities with far more patients than staff could easily manage.

Several additional factors seem to have contributed to the demise of moral treatment. By the middle of the century the leaders of the moral treatment movement were aged or had died, and they appear to have left very few students to carry on their work. At the same time there was a shift in the accepted understanding of mental illness. The romantic period, during which moral treatment had blossomed, came to an end to be replaced by a new positivism with its emphasis on the importance of the facts and certitudes of the hard sciences. At the same time the centers of thought and leadership in psychiatry moved from the hospitals to the universities. Mental illness came to be viewed as an organic problem, and the moral treatment movement came to an end. In the words of Almond:

> It is sobering to realize that a hospital reform movement with international scope could give way over a few decades to custodial, dehumanizing patterns of care that are still reflected in many of our state hospitals.[6]

Those changes in thought and culture and their impact on moral treatment are discussed in more detail later in this chapter.

Milieu Therapy Movement

The next innovative period in psychiatric hospital care began during the early decades of the twentieth century. This movement, later known as the milieu therapy movement, was also international in scope. Its primary concern was to create a social environment in the hospital, and sometimes outside it, that supported the patients' treatment and recovery.

During the first two decades of the twentieth century Herman Simon,[7] a German psychiatrist, developed a form of treatment called *activere behandlung,* which, translated literally, means *more active therapy.* Simon hypothesized that patients' behaviors were responsive to the expectations of those around them. From this he developed a treatment that included not only an assessment of the patient's pathology but also an assessment of the patient's recent and past work performance. The patient was then given tasks to perform based on that assessment. The patient learned each task step by step with help and encouragement from a staff person. When the patient successfully completed a particular task he or she was encouraged to perform another more difficult one.

In helping the patients perform their tasks, Simon enlisted the help of all the staff. He believed that it was important to maintain among both patients and staff an atmosphere that supported recovery and good functioning.

Simon's treatment became known as *milieutherapie,* and by the 1920s was well known throughout Germany until it ceased with the rise of Fascism. Fortunately, as happened with moral treatment, milieutherapie developed concurrently in other countries.

Adolf Aichhorn,[8] an educator and disciple of Freud, used the social structure as part of his treatment plan for institutionalized adolescents at Hollabrun, Austria. Aichhorn used the peer relationships that developed among the adolescents and the transferences they experienced toward the counselors to bring about change.

By the 1930s the movement spread to the United States. One example is the work of the Menninger brothers,[9] who introduced the *milieu therapy* of Germany to the Menninger Foundation in Topeka, Kansas.

In brief, milieu treatment recognized the importance of human relationships in sustaining mental health and used the social environment of the hospital, or aspects of it, to support patients' treatment and recovery. Typically, a patient's psychiatrist told the hospital staff, on the basis of knowledge gained from individual therapy, what kind of social interactions would be most beneficial to the patient. If the patient was depressed, for example, the psychiatrist might recommend an attitude of firm kindness. In turn, the staff kept the psychiatrist informed about the effectiveness of those directives, which could then be modified to meet the patient's needs better.

Although milieu therapy's development may have been hampered by World War II, unlike the moral therapy movement, it did not come to an end. Variations of milieu therapy are still actively pursued in a variety of inpatient psychiatric settings.

THERAPEUTIC COMMUNITY MOVEMENT

The therapeutic community and the milieu therapy movements are often confused with each other. That is understandable because they have a number of overlapping characteristics. For example, both forms of treatment acknowledge the importance and therapeutic usefulness of some, if not all, aspects of the patient's hospital experience. But there are sufficient differences, both philosophically and historically, to warrant considering them separate movements.

The central tenets of the therapeutic community movement emphasized the healing potential of each member of the community including the patients, of all relationships within the community, and of the community as a whole.[10–12] For the leaders of the movement certain practices followed from those tenets. First, there was a high degree of egalitarianism among the staff and between staff and patients. Many treatment and community management decisions were made jointly by staff and patients. They included decisions regarding the use of medication, attendance at groups, receiving off-ground privileges, and so on. In addition, each patient was expected to take responsibility for his or her own treatment. Patients usually entered a hospital with the expectation that others would cure them. It was a goal of the therapeutic community to alter that expectation and place the responsibility on the patient.[13]

Second, all patient interactions in the hospital were included in the treatment process. It was assumed that patients' difficulties and characteristic ways of relating would be revealed in whatever they did in the hospital, thus all exchanges among patients and between patients and staff were seen as opportunities for understanding patient difficulties and encouraging new ways of behaving. Because of the importance placed on relationships, groups became a central part of the therapeutic community. Group treatment included a variety of meetings and activities, such as group therapy, patient government meetings, family group meetings, job training meetings, ward meetings, addiction groups, and so on. The kind of group meetings a particular hospital used depended on the patient population and the staff's interests and skills. Individual therapy was often secondary to those meetings or existed as a means of reinforcing the groups and the community esprit de corps, or both.

Third, all of the above were seen as means of creating a therapeutic culture in the hospital. The community-as-a-whole emerged as a healing instrument, which, in turn, reinforced the other treatments. The central body that represented the coming together of all the treatments and reflected the community's healing function was the community meeting, which was comprised of all staff members and patients. The same egalitarian spirit pervaded this meeting as it did in other parts of the hospital. Staff and patients were expected to participate and use it to facilitate the day-to-day working of the community and the healing of the patients.

Although egalitarianism was espoused in the therapeutic community movement, it did not mean that the staff was relieved of authority, rather it "remains latent to be evoked when necessary."[14] That was usually when patients' limitations rendered them unable to bear their responsibilities adequately.

Maxwell Jones' industrial rehabilitation unit at Belmont Hospital, England, is viewed as the official birthplace of the therapeutic community movement.[15] Jones' example spread very rapidly in England and North America where his model found expression in the work of Sullivan,[16,17] the Cummings,[18] and others. A number of factors seem to have contributed to the rapid growth of the therapeutic community approach.

World War II effected many major social changes and shifts in perspectives and values in the Western World including the world of mental health care. Work with the military, for instance, revealed much more of the scope of emotional illness among the general population. Paradoxically, a shortage of staff in mental hospitals during the war showed how effectively those institutions could be run by a limited staff with the help of the patients themselves. The effectiveness of milieu therapy before and after the war also encouraged the use of the hospital community as a therapeutic tool. These new learnings, allied to the new optimism following World War II regarding the treatment of emotional disorders, greatly facilitated the spread of the work of Jones and others. Writing in the United States, Jerome Frank observed:

> Ever since World War II, mental hospitals have been undergoing
> a quiet but massive revolution from essentially custodial institutions
> to active treatment centres, involving progressive breakdown of the

barrier between the mental hospital and the community and a re-definition of the roles of patients and treatment staff within the hospital walls.[19]

The therapeutic community as we have defined it refers specifically to those modes of hospital treatment that follow Jones' model. It is worth noting, however, that others have used the term, particularly in England,[20] more broadly than we have here. Some have used it to include any treatment that makes use of the hospital environment[21] and others have considered it a special case of milieu therapy.[22,23] There is also evidence that Main[24] may have used the term prior to Jones, and Foulkes[25] has claimed that the treatment model that he and his colleagues practiced at Northfield Military Hospital in England was the first therapeutic community. Others have suggested that the "total push" treatment in the United States,[26,27] which used all the staff to try to bring about change in patients, may have been the earliest example of the therapeutic community movement. The truth about these matters may always remain clouded. More than likely there was a growing interest among a number of practitioners in the field at this time about using the social environment in a more egalitarian way.

THE PSYCHODYNAMIC THREAD

The three movements described have focused, in different ways, on the role of the hospital environment in effecting change. But other change agents also have been applied. In recent years, psychoactive drugs have had a major impact on inpatient care and have been used by staff to bring a variety of symptomatology and bizarre behaviors under control. Behavior therapy has been used in a similar way. Psychoanalytically trained therapists have also brought their learning and skills into the psychiatric hospital. The latter group is of particular relevance to this book.

Psychoanalytically oriented psychotherapy or "psychodynamic psychotherapy" entered the psychiatric hospital around the beginning of the milieu therapy movement. We observed earlier that Aichhorn used transference along with milieu therapy techniques with his adolescent patients in Austria. Since that time psychodynamic psychotherapy has been practiced in a number of well-known psychiatric institutions in the United States, such as Chestnut Lodge in Maryland, Austin Riggs in Massachusetts, and the Menninger Foundation in Kansas. Harry Stack Sullivan and his followers also practiced psychodynamic psychotherapy with severely ill patients in which they placed a particular emphasis on the role of interpersonal relations.[28–30] Psychodynamic psychotherapy also has been practiced fairly widely in academic hospitals where psychiatric residents and others are being trained. Psychodynamic psychotherapy has contributed significantly to the treatment and understanding of severe emotional illnesses. We discuss that contribution in more detail in Chapter 2.

MORAL TREATMENT, MILIEU THERAPY, AND THERAPEUTIC COMMUNITY MOVEMENT IN CONTEXT

The approaches to the hospital care of the mentally ill that we have just described were the fruit of the social and cultural environments of their time, and shared many of their assumptions about life. To understand those approaches more fully, we now discuss the environments out of which they emerged. Much of the material that follows is based on the work of Ellenberger[31] and Russell.[32]

There were five, often overlapping, social and cultural movements that arose during the period we are discussing. They were triggered by the industrial and scientific revolutions of the time. They were the Enlightenment, Romanticism, Positivism, Marxism, and Darwinism. These movements placed differing emphases on the importance of thinking and feeling, and of the individual and the society or group in human affairs.

The enlightenment, which began around 1730, elevated reason to a position of supremacy, considering it to be a "permanent universal entity, which was the same for all men of all ages and all countries."[33] Man was also viewed as a social being and society was created for him. Thus, the ideal person was someone whose life was directed by the requirements of reason and society. Authority lost its power and was replaced by science and the use of analysis, as in mathematics, as ways of understanding and managing the world. Emotions were viewed as disturbances of the rational mind, passions were considered tyrannous, and fantasies were suspect. Science promised a great new world and was to be used for the benefit of all. Humankind was on the march and with the use of science and reason progress was sure to follow. Conversely, progress was confirmation of the value of reason. It was a period of optimism, intellectual and religious tolerance, and social concern.

The enlightenment had a major impact on medicine having introduced "pediatrics, orthopedics, public hygiene,"[34] and small pox inoculations. Within the area of mental health its major contribution lay in the reform of mental hospitals as reflected in the work of men such as Pinel and Tuke, mentioned earlier.

Romanticism arose in the early 1800s as a reaction to the enlightenment. Romanticism elevated feelings and the irrational to positions of supremacy while reason took a secondary position. The individual was also elevated and the eccentricities, particularly the emotional ones, of the individual were enlarged and accepted. Rather than view the individual as being guided by society, the Romantics viewed society as something from which the individual needed to escape. Nevertheless, they also placed a great deal of importance on the value of friendships and other close relationships. The ideal person was someone of extreme sensitivity enabling him or her "to 'feel into' Nature and to 'feel with' other men," having "a rich inner life, belief in the power of inspiration, intuition and spontaneity"[35] and in the importance of the emotional life. It was an era of great passion, of the power of love over status, and of the value of nature over everyday commerce and business. Progress was not a process determined by reason. Rather human life was a process of spontaneous unfolding, "a series of metamorphoses."[36]

Within the field of mental health, it was also an era that gave rise to the exploration of the irrational and the unconscious, to the study of dreams and fantasy, to the development of psychotherapy and psychodrama. It was an era that highlighted the importance of psychology in the creation and cure of illness. The leaders in this field included men such as Reil,[37] Iderer,[38] and Neumann.[39] As Ellenberger ably illustrates, the work of these men is strikingly similar to that of Freud and Jung and later dynamic psychologists.

Thus, although the intellectual fervor and social awareness of the enlightenment gave moral treatment its birth, romanticism gave it its nourishment. The enlightenment signaled the death knell of witchcraft and possession as the causes of mental illness and romanticism brought to light the role of the inner world of the patient. It was these cultural environments that gave moral treatment its basic assumptions and informed its actions.

In the early days of the moral treatment movement this meant an international wave of hospital reform. But it also meant practices such as cold-water dousings and the use of painful straightjackets to manipulate patients into rational behavior and to control the passions that were so abhorrent to the men of the enlightenment. But, with the greater acceptance of affective intensity during the romantic period, other aspects of treatment became emphasized. The insane were treated, "so far as their condition will possibly admit, as if they were still in the enjoyment of the healthy exercise of their mental faculties."[40] To attain this goal they were to be given as much freedom as was consistent with their safety and the safety of others. In these assumptions and practices is the integration of the social responsibility of the enlightenment and the acceptance and valuing of the individual freedom and passions of the romantics.

The cultural movements that followed the enlightenment and the romantic periods have been movements that, among other things, emphasized particular aspects of those two counterpunctal periods. For instance, positivism, which followed the romantic period, was a return to the emphasis on reason and science of the enlightenment.

Positivists searched for the certitude that came from experimentation and knowing the facts. They did not speculate about the nature of things; their primary interests were in applied science and in that which was useful. They were, however, very concerned with man as a social being, the study of which led to the development of the science of sociology. The ideal person of the positivist period was the scientist often caricatured as the "savant." The savant was the classic absent-minded professor and researcher. His most salient feature was a general attitude of disinterestedness.

Such an environment was fertile ground for the establishment of the "somatiker." Two psychiatric trends had been apparent since the beginning of the nineteenth century. In Germany they were called the somatiker and the psychiker. The psychiker, who emphasized the psychological causes of mental illness, was in ascendancy during the romantic period and in the moral treatment movement. During the period of positivism the somatiker, who attributed mental diseases to physical causes, was in ascendancy. A few psychikers remained, such as Fechner[41] and Bachofen,[42] but they were the exception; the more common orientation was that declared by Griesinger, "mental diseases are brain diseases."[43] Despite the statement credited to Griesinger, he tried to integrate the psychological and the biological in his own work. But, the psychological aspects of his work were generally overlooked by his successors, including such leading psychiatrists as Westphal,[44] Meynert,[45] and Wernicke.[46] During this period important strides were made in understanding brain functioning and in differentiating various types of mental disorders that culminated in the work of Kraepelin.[47] It was also during this period that the major centers of psychiatry moved from the hospital to the university, which had become the center for scientific research. The fertile ground for the somatiker, however, proved to be fallow for the moral treatment movement, which came to an end, and mental hospitals once again became places of confinement rather than places of healing.[48]

Some aspects of this movement are also reflected in the work of Freud. He emphasized the importance of biological causality, and the importance of a disinterested stance on the part of the analyst toward the analysand. As Ellenberger notes,[49] Freud seems to have integrated aspects of all the movements occurring in the latter half of the nineteenth century. The greatest influence upon Freud, however, seems to have been the neo-romantic movement, which we discuss shortly.

Two other movements that appeared during the second half of the nineteenth century deserve brief comment. They were Darwinism and Marxism. These movements struggled with two issues that were important during both the enlightenment and romantic periods: namely progress and the role of society in human life.

Darwin's discoveries were turned by others into a variety of philosophies of life for both good and ill. It is sufficient for us to note that his work led to a renewed interest in, and gave new meaning to, progress. Darwin viewed the evolution of human society as the result of the "instinct of sympathy and mutual help between animals of the same species."[50] Some followers emphasized the element of chance, and the blind universal struggle in evolution, whereas others used such interpretations as rationale for war and destruction, and ruthless competition. Later, Freud used the instinct and sexual theories of Plato, Darwin, and others in developing his own personality system.[51]

Marx placed a different focus on the role of progress in society. For many of Darwin's followers progress was instinctual and mechanical, whereas for Marx it was a dialectic process to be aided by man's efforts. Man was alienated from himself because of the division of society into classes, in which the ruling class oppresses and exploits the rest. Thus, he argued, a classless society would remove the alienation. For our purposes, the important distinction to note is a renewed emphasis on the importance and role of society (or the group) in human development. For Marx and his followers, if the society could be restructured people would be happier and no longer alienated, an orientation similar to that of the therapeutic community movement.

As the nineteenth century ended, the impact of these movements was greatly modified by a resurgence of romanticism, sometimes referred to as neo-romanticism. Neo-romanticism arose as a reaction against positivism and bore many of the characteristics of the earlier romanticism. There was a renewed interest in the irrational, in mysticism, in dreams, in the unconscious, and in the role of psychology in mental illness. There was also a great deal of interest in understanding sexuality and challenging sexual mores, particularly among the wealthier classes. Neo-romanticism differed in some important ways from the earlier romanticism. Romanticism had emphasized the uniqueness of each individual, seeing him at the same time in the context of interpersonal relations with friends, colleagues, lovers, and family. Neo-romanticism stressed the worship of the individual to the point where he was isolated from others. As Ellenberger points out "the Narcissus figure was a general symbol and incarnation of the spirit of that time."[52] Romanticism had viewed everything as in a process of growth and evolution. Neo-romanticism viewed everything as in a process of decay that lead to speculations about the universality of a death instinct.

Neo-romanticism was fertile ground for the psychiker. He reappeared through men such as Forel, Meyer, Bleuler, Freud, Jung, and Adler. With the return of interest in the role of psychology in mental illness it was not long before the effects were being felt in the mental hospitals. During this period the milieu therapy movement had its start, and the relationship between the therapist and the patient was given renewed importance. Additionally, psychoanalytic thinking and techniques, which were also strongly influenced by the spirit of the times, were being introduced to inpatient settings.

A variety of socialist movements, some Marxist in orientation and some not, also were very active in the early part of the twentieth century, particularly in Europe. The strongest Marxist influence was felt in Eastern Europe, but Western Europe also was affected. Following World War II Britain elected a socialist (Labour) government and implemented a wide variety of social programs based on the assumption that the society was responsible for the care of its members. That belief was reflected in the slogan "from each according to his ability, to each according to his need." Such a cultural ethos also affected the field of mental health. One of those effects was the development of the therapeutic community movement with its particular emphasis on the community as a healing organism.

The cultural movements we have reviewed continue to impact on the treatment of mental illness. In some inpatient settings a romantic (psychological–psychoanalytic) influence holds sway, in others an enlightenment/positivist (biological–behavioral) influence, in yet others there is an integration of the various movements. What new cultural movement is currently impinging on our treatment of mental illness and the running of our psychiatric hospitals is difficult to say. Cultural movements are best described after they have taken place and are nigh impossible to describe by those who are living during them. Having made that caveat, we will make an observation about our current treatment of mental illness.

Relativity, systems theory, and ecology are becoming part of our everyday language. They reflect a new way of viewing the world, a view that moves away from that of linear causality and mechanistic approaches to mental illness and its treatment toward a multicausal and interactive approach. Such an approach makes possible an integration of the biological, psychological, interpersonal, and social causes and cures of mental illness. In Chapters 3, 4, and 5 we discuss how such an orientation can also facilitate our understanding and management of a psychiatric unit and of the psychotherapy groups in that unit.

In the meantime we turn to a review of the history of inpatient psychotherapy groups.

HISTORY OF INPATIENT GROUP PSYCHOTHERAPY

The history of inpatient group therapy is closely interwoven with the history of the hospital reform movements. What was fertile ground for one seems to have been fertile ground for the other. In some instances one was an essential ingredient of the other as in the therapeutic community. Many of the early pioneers of group therapy began their group practice in inpatient settings.

The person generally credited with beginning group therapy in the United States was Joseph H. Pratt. Dr. Pratt began his work in 1905, which was around the time the milieu therapy movement had its start. There are indications, however, that group therapy may have been practiced as much as a century earlier during the era of moral treatment.

In 1803 Johann Reil described various "psychic" methods that could be used in a Tollhaus (Lunacy Asylum) – a name he suggested should be changed – to help people with mental illness. He described one procedure as follows:

> Among these methods is that of the "therapeutic theatre" in which the employees of the institution will play various roles, and where the patients will also be given parts in accordance with their specific conditions.[53]

The similarity with modern psychodrama is striking, as indeed are some of the healing practices of primitive societies,[54] suggesting that the use of the group as a method of healing has a long and honored history.

The resurgence of interest in using the group as an instrument of healing, however, began early in this century. Pratt was an internist working with tuberculosis patients in Boston, Massachusetts. Tuberculosis was a social as well as a physical problem. Patients were frequently shunned because of their illness and Pratt's patients were no exception. They were demoralized. With money raised by a local pastor, Dr. Pratt developed classes for his patients. These classes usually had about twenty to thirty members, although the actual number attending each meeting was about fifteen. The classes met twice weekly in the homes of the members. In these classes Dr. Pratt taught his patients about their illness, its onset, course, and cure. Patients who had responded successfully to treatment shared their experiences with the group. Patients who were particularly resistant to treatment had individual sessions with a nurse who was known as a "friendly advisor."[55] The most salient features of these meetings were their camaraderie, support, and hope.[56]

In 1919 a similar approach was used by L. Cody Marsh with institutionalized psychiatric patients. Marsh began work in a mental hospital as a minister. He felt that more could be done for the patients than was being done, so he entered medical school and became a physician. Later he returned to work in Worcester State Hospital in Worcester, Massachusetts, where he used the public address system to give talks to the patients. He also formed discussion groups on the wards for the patients and had similar sessions with hospital personnel at all levels. Marsh's group sessions with the patients were similar to those of Pratt. He called them classes and lectured the patients on the origins and manifestations of mental illness. A record was kept of each patient's attendance, punctuality, and attentiveness. The patients were expected to sit and pass an examination on the course. If the patient did poorly he may have had to re-sit the examination, which was given several times a year. If a patient had particular difficulty he could be given an individual tutor. Marsh's motto was "By the crowd they have been broken, by the crowd they can be healed."[57-59]

Group sessions with staff included physicians, nurses, social workers, and aides. Marsh believed that the social environment was particularly important to the health and cure of the patient and felt it was important that the staff understand the nature of the patients' difficulties and relate to them in a humane manner. He also encouraged all his staff to be actively involved in the care of the patients. Because of this, some consider him to be the originator of the therapeutic community model, predating the work of Maxwell Jones.

Around this time, Lazell[60] was meeting with hospitalized schizophrenic patients in groups. Like Marsh, he lectured to the patients on the nature of their illness. Lazell went farther than Marsh by teaching patients the basic concepts of psychoanalysis. Within this framework he tried to develop an understanding of why meeting in classes was helpful. He argued that his patients improved, in part, because their fears were reduced through education. He also believed that the process of patients getting to know one another in their classes contributed to their improvement. He observed that many of his patients, often perceived as being otherwise inaccessible, retained the information given in the lectures and that much of the conversation that took place between the patients after the lectures included sharing of information and comparing of symptoms.[61] Those are important ingredients in the formation of any group or personal relationship.

In Switzerland,* beginning in the early 1900s, the directors of psychiatric hospitals, including leading psychiatrists, such as Klaesi in Berne,[62] E. and M. Bleuler in Zurich,[63] and J. E. Staehelin in Basel,[64] organized a rural family-care system that used primary groups within the community for the treatment of severe mental illness. A primary group included a rural family of parents and children and all those who worked on their farm. In these settings, under the occasional supervision of an attendant or social worker, the patients enjoyed the countryside, gradually made contact with those around them and were encouraged to carry out some light work on their own. Group therapy in this instance meant incorporating patients into well-functioning groups outside the hospital. The host families provided these patients with a supportive family group

---

* Most of the material on group therapy in Switzerland in this chapter comes from a private interview with Dr. Raymond Battegay at the American Group Psychotherapy Association annual conference in New York, February 1985. Dr. Battegay has been a world leader in the field of group psychotherapy for many years and is Chief of the University Out-Patient Clinic, Chairman and Professor of Psychiatry, University of Basel, Basel, Switzerland.

Many people have contributed to the growth of inpatient group psychotherapy from a variety of countries. Unfortunately, much of their work has gone unrecorded. For this reason the authors are particularly grateful to Dr. Battegay for his willingness to help us in this area.

in which they could belong, in contrast with many of their own families who did not want them.

From 1933 to 1945, with the rise of Nazism, psychiatry and group treatments declined in Germany, where psychiatric patients were frequently killed rather than treated. By contrast, Switzerland was one of the few countries in Europe that maintained its democratic and psychiatric institutions during this period. Here inpatient group psychotherapy continued, particularly in affiliation with occupational therapy. The occupational therapy groups played an enormous role in rehabilitating patients, especially schizophrenic patients.[65]

In the United States, Wender[66] practiced group psychotherapy in inpatient settings in the late 1920s and the 1930s with patients whom we would probably call borderline today. He used psychoanalytic concepts and took pains to distinguish his group methods from the work of others who used educational and directive techniques. He believed that for his method to be successful patients had to have some degree of affect present and be free of intellectual impairment. Male and female patients were treated in separate groups. In addition he strongly recommended that patients have individual therapy along with group therapy.

Wender believed that the group was a recreation of the family. The members viewed the therapist as a symbolic parent and each other as siblings. This gave the members a chance to rework some of their unresolved family conflicts.

In 1936 Schilder[67] described groups he led at Bellevue Hospital, New York, based on psychodynamic principles. Schilder used Wender's concept of the group as a recreation of the family. He also emphasized the importance of the free associations that took place in the group between and among members. He argued that when one patient recalled a particular event in his family of origin other members often recalled similar experiences or feelings. Such sharing enabled patients to realize that they were not alone, and reduced the feelings of isolation.

During World War II group therapy was practiced in a number of military hospitals. One such hospital was Northfield Military Hospital in Northfield, England. In that setting Bion,[68] Foulkes,[69] Ezriel,[70] and Main[71] developed their various approaches to group therapy. Foulkes later described the theoretical and technical conclusions he drew from that work and how they could be applied in a civilian setting.[72,73]

Foulkes used psychoanalytic concepts as guides to understanding and leading a variety of groups including psychotherapy groups, activity groups, spontaneous peer groups formed by patients who were doing the same work, or sleeping in the same part of the hospital, and task groups that were formed to solve particular problems within the hospital unit, such as making the staging for a show or getting together a band for a celebration.

Foulkes placed particular emphasis on the healing qualities of the group as a whole and believed it was the leader's task to facilitate that process. In this model, the leader may be quite active to get things going and help establish relationships among the members, but should then gradually move into the background and permit the group to do its own healing. He recognized that inpatient group members usually look to the leader for a "cure," so that the task of enabling the group to take responsibility for itself and its members is not an easy one. He wrote:

> To get them actively engaged and in a state of spontaneous par-ticipation is uphill work indeed . . . however, . . . It is remarkable how much keenness and ingenuity the same group will display, and how much unexpected talent, intelligence, interest, experience, rich emotional life, humor and even wisdom or genius can be found in every group.[74]

Foulkes was also acutely aware of the complex interrelationship between the group and the hospital unit. He observed how the groups he began influenced the whole hospital so that, in time, the hospital became viewed as a large therapeutic group of which his small groups were a part. By the same token he noted how group life was profoundly affected by that larger community. He describes the paradoxical change in morale that took place, first in the hospital and then in his groups, when World War II came to an end. At that point the goal of treatment changed from preparing men to return to the war to preparing them to return to civilian life. The hospital staff became depleted by demobili-zation and morale dropped. The groups were unable to function effec-tively until Foulkes found a way of raising the hospital's morale again.[75] Thus, for Foulkes, there were continuous, reciprocal relationships among the individual members of the group, the group, and the hospital com-munity. He wrote:

> The conviction that man's neuroses and their treatment change their form decisively in accordance with the community in which they arise is fundamental for a group approach. . . . I could observe how patients' minds, concerns, attitudes and even symptoms, changed according to the dynamics of the hospital as a whole.[76]

Although Foulkes is better known for his work as a group therapist, contrary to common wisdom,† he viewed his work at Northfield as the development of the first therapeutic community.

Group therapy was used in other settings in England around this time and need only be mentioned at this point to illustrate the growth of this treatment method. They included Netherne Hospital, Warlingham Park, Cassel Hospital, Ingrebourne Centre, and Belmont Hospital. It is also worth noting that all these hospitals were based on the therapeutic community model.

In Europe, following World War II, outpatient group therapy was practiced in Biel/Bienne, Switzerland by Friedemann[77] and later, in the early 1950s, in Basel, Switzerland by Battegay.[78] In 1953, encouraged by Friedemann, Battegay began working with large inpatient groups of 15 to 25 patients from the same ward, making him the first person in Switzerland to practice group therapy in a hospital setting. In the beginning, he read short fairy tales to the group members, such as those written by the brothers Grimm or by Hans Christian Andersen. The stories were usually chosen to match the particular needs of the patients. After the reading of the stories, the patients talked about the relationship of the stories to their concerns. In time, he stopped using the fairy tales and used whatever material arose spontaneously from the members, following the psychodynamic model. In 1957 Battegay also began leading smaller inpatient groups of 5 to 7 patients with the same psychiatric illness. The object of these small, diagnostically homogeneous groups was to amplify the patients' emotions and stimulate insight into their unconscious motives and needs, on the one hand, while providing social learning and support from people with similar difficulties, on the other.

Like some of the early pioneers in inpatient groups, Battegay strongly believed in the importance of the other staff members in the treatment of patients. Also, like Freud, he believed in the importance of the therapist having an understanding of his own dynamics. With these matters in mind he provided groups for the hospital staff. First, he led groups for nurses on the staff and for nurses from the hospital's nurses' school. Later he led groups for the psychiatrists, numbers of whom had been in psychoanalysis.

In the United States there was a similar growth in the use of group therapy following World War II. Moreno, the father of psychodrama, may be viewed as an important link between the group therapy of Europe

---

† See p. 6.

and that of the United States. Moreno began his work in Europe and was probably the first person to use the term group psychotherapy.[79] He came to the United States in 1925 where he worked actively in the field of group therapy until his death in 1974. By 1953 Corsini, describing the growth of psychodrama in inpatient settings, noted that "more than 30 psychodrama stages have been constructed in mental hospitals, the first at St. Elizabeth's in Washington; . . ."[80]

In the early decades following World War II, many other therapists, besides Moreno and his followers, practiced group therapy in inpatient settings in the United States. An illustration from the New England area will be sufficient to demonstrate the kind of work done.

In Boston, Semrad began therapy groups based on psychodynamic principles and encouraged his colleagues and psychiatry residents at Boston State Hospital to do likewise. Those colleagues and residents included Drs. Doris Menzer-Benaron‡ and Max Day.[81–84] In describing Semrad's work, Menzer-Benaron recalled that in the late 1940s Boston State Hospital was like a large warehouse for the storage of mental patients. Day described it as ". . . a total absolute mess, worse than the state hospitals that have been exposed in the national press."[85] Semrad first provided individual psychotherapy for some of the chronic patients in which he tried "to understand the human being."[86] But it soon became clear that there were not enough therapists available to provide individual treatment for the large numbers of patients at the hospital. So he turned to groups.

There were two major categories of patients at the hospital, those whose illness had become chronic and those whose illness was acute. The acute patients were usually those who had been referred by the courts for evaluation and possibly treatment, whereas the chronic patients had been living in the hospital, often for many years. Much of the group therapy that was practiced by Semrad and his staff was conducted with the chronic patients. Because the patients were housed in male and female wards, the groups were also divided along sexual lines.

---

‡ Much of the material on the work at Boston State Hospital was gained through a private interview with Dr. Doris Menzer-Benaron at her home in Newton, Massachusetts, in March 1985. Just as in other parts of the world, much of the work being done in inpatient group therapy in the early post World War II years in the United States and in Boston was not recorded. So the authors are very grateful that Dr. Menzer-Benaron took the time to tell us.

Some of the theoretical material that grew out of that period is recorded in articles published by Semrad and Day. Some examples of that work have been included in the references at the end of the chapter.

Leading groups of chronic patients was a difficult and often frustrating task. Patients were often unresponsive and on occasion got out of control. And at that time there was very little medication to assist the therapist in the task. Menzer-Benaron recalls that what facilitated dialogue within those chronic groups was being able to address patients' "conflict free areas of the ego." Once, for instance, she sat at a table with a group of men with whom she had been unable to make any verbal contact despite many tries. In the middle of the table was a radio broadcasting a baseball game. She turned to the patient next to her and asked him to teach her about the game. He did. As he described the game others listened, then began to join in. And so the group began. After numbers of sessions in which the members taught the leader, they began to listen to what she had to say. They took her advice about how to get day passes from the hospital, how to contact their relatives, and so on. In time they began to dress well and to clean up the ward to impress their young, attractive doctor.

In response to the demands of the task, the therapists at Boston State developed their own support group in which they talked about their work and shared their experiences. They also observed each other leading groups.

ANALYSIS OF THE HISTORY OF INPATIENT GROUP THERAPY

Many of the inpatient groups at the beginning of the twentieth century may be described, using Thomas'[87] and Hulse's[88] terminology, as repressive–inspirational, didactic, and highly directive, whereas those following World War II were often analytic and much less directive in their approach. Groups led by Pratt, Marsh, and Lazell, for instance, were often referred to as classes and included lectures related to the patients' disorders. Sometimes they included examinations. Lecturing about emotional or physical disorders, and evaluating the amount of information received reduced regression and reinforced repression. At the same time, many of those lectures were used to inspire hope and encouragement for the patients. Rosenbaum, in describing the work of Marsh, wrote that he "used almost a religious revival technique, which was very inspirational."[89]

Wender[90] and Schilder[91] used psychoanalytic concepts in leading their inpatient groups during the 1930s and may be viewed as representing a transition between the educational and inspirational models of the earlier part of the century and the more analytical models of the latter half of the century.

Groups led by Foulkes,[92] Bion,[93] Battegay,[94] and Semrad and Day[95] were clearly analytical and introspective in their approach. These leaders emphasized the spontaneous interactions among the members, the development of transference, and the analysis and interpretation of those transferences and of their group behavior. As a rule, they did not pass information on to the group members about the nature of their illnesses.

Although there does appear to be a general trend over the years from the inspirational and didactic to the analytical, not all groups fit neatly into that trend. The work of Moreno, for example, which began early in the century, has features of both ends of this continuum and others that are unique to psychodrama. His work may be viewed as analytical in that it sought to isolate a central problem of a patient, have it played out on a stage, and worked through. Like the analytical stance, he encouraged spontaneity, albeit in behavior as well as in words. But his method was also highly directive. The therapist arranged the staging, the parts, and the players, and often determined who should speak to whom.

The inpatient groups of the earlier part of the century differed in other ways from those that appeared later. As one would expect, inpatient groups have become more formalized over time.[96] The early groups were experimental and idiosyncratic. Often they were developed in response to the overwhelming demands of providing adequate treatment to a large number of patients with inadequate numbers of staff.[97] Thus groups varied in size and composition. Pratt's groups had up to twenty-five members, whereas Marsh had several hundred in his.[98] Pratt's groups were homogeneous, being made up of tuberculosis patients, whereas Marsh's groups were made up of all the patients on the floor.

Since World War II, there has been much greater formalization of inpatient group therapy. There is general agreement, for instance, that, more often than not, an inpatient group has eight to ten members sitting in a circle, that the group lasts from forty-five to ninety minutes, and has one or two leaders. Often, the members of the group are encouraged to interact spontaneously with one another, and that spontaneity provides the material for the group session.

Concomitantly, there has been a growth in theory building about, and in the refinement of technique for, inpatient groups, much of it along psychodynamic lines. Examples of this growth in theory building are reflected in the work of Foulkes,[99] Klein,[100] Kibel,[101] Rice and Rutan,[102] Lonergan,[103] Yalom,[104] Hannah,[105] and Maxmen[106] among others. Thus, although differences continue to exist among leaders of inpatient groups, those differences are usually differences around formalized ways of leading groups, that is, differences between "schools." For instance, Foulkes and his colleagues emphasize the healing capacity of the group qua group, whereas Yalom and his colleagues, emphasize the healing capacity of the interpersonal interactions within the group. In contrast to Foulkes, Yalom places little emphasis on the role of the group qua group in inpatient settings. Rather he views each group session as relatively autonomous from those preceding it and those following it.

Many of the changes that have taken place in inpatient group therapy since the beginning of this century, as Dreikurs and Corsini noted,[107] also reflect the growing democratization of Western society during the period. As in society at large, there has been a shift from authoritarian leadership in group to a more egalitarian relationship between the members and the therapist so that the members usually determine the direction a session will take.

Although changes in the therapists' styles and techniques have taken place over the years, current inpatient groups share many common elements with their predecessors. Most of the groups reviewed created an atmosphere that fostered caring, support, and mutual helping among the members. That fact was true whether the groups were didactic or analytical. For instance, after Lasell's[108] "classes" the members gathered around and talked about their common experiences. That is, they learned they were not alone as did members of Foulkes'[109] psychodynamic groups. Other elements strongly emphasized in the earlier inpatient groups also can be seen in current inpatient groups, but their source is different. It has been our experience in leading psychodynamic groups that the members often provide inspiration, hope, and education for each other just as the early therapists did for their group members. This is often done by one member, who is feeling better, encouraging other members to "hang in there," telling them that he once felt as badly as they do now. Sometimes this encouragement is followed by a description of how he got better or of how best to use the hospital and the group to improve.

Given the common features observed in groups over the years, the question to be addressed is, how does the inpatient psychodynamic therapist address and use those commonalities for healing?

REFERENCES

1. R. Almond, *The Healing Community* (New York: Jason Aronson, 1974), p. xxxiii.

2. J. Morrisset, H. Goldman, and L. Klerman, *The Enduring Asylum: Cycles of Institutional Reform at Worcester State Hospital* (New York: Grune and Stratton, 1980).

3. J. S. Bockoven, *Moral Treatment in Community Mental Health* (New York: Springer, 1972) pp. 12–13.

4. G. F. Blandford, *Insanity and its Treatment* (New York: William Wood and Co., 1883).

5. *Ibid.*, pp. 38–39.

6. Almond, *The Healing Community*, p. xxxix.

7. H. Simon, "Activere Krankenbehandlung in der Irrenanstatt," *I, II, III, Allgemeine Zeitschrift fur Psychiatrie* 87 (Nov. 15, 1927): 97; 90a (May 1929): 69; 90b (July 4, 1929): 245.

8. Almond, *The Healing Community*, p. xli.

9. W. C. Menninger, "The Psychoanalytic Principles Applied to the Treatment of Hospitalized Patients," *Bull. Menninger Clin.* (1936):35–43.

10. H. A. Wilmer, "Toward a Definition of the Therapeutic Community," *Am. J. Psychiatry* 114 (1958):824–834.

11. K. L. Artiss, *Milieu Therapy in Schizophrenia* (New York: Grune & Stratton, 1962).

12. D. Daniels and R. Rubin, "The Community Meeting," *Arch. Gen. Environ. Therapy* 18 (1968):60–75.

13. J. Cumming and E. Cumming, *Ego and Milieu: Theory and Practice of Environmental Therapy* (New York: Atherton, 1962).

14. M. Jones, "Community Psychiatry," in *Modern Perspectives in World Psychiatry*. Vol 2, edited by J. G. Howells (New York: Brunner/Mazel, 1971), p. 692.

15. M. Jones, *The Therapeutic Community* (New York: Basic Books, 1953).

16. H. S. Sullivan, "Environmental Factors and Course Under Treatment of Schizophrenia," *Med. J. Record* 1 (1933):19–22.

17. H. S. Sullivan, "Sociopsychiatric Research: Its Implications for the Schizophrenia Problem and For Mental Hygiene," *Am. J. Psychiatry* 10 (1931):977–991.

18. Cummings and Cummings, *Ego and Milieu: Theory and Practice of Environmental Therapy*.

19. J. D. Frank, *Persuasion and Healing*. (Baltimore & London: The John Hopkins University Press, 1973), p. 297.

20. T. F. Main, "The Hospital as a Therapeutic Institution," *Bull. Menninger Clin.* 10 (1946):66–70.

21. S. J. Korchin, *Modern Clinical Psychology*. (New York: Basic Books, 1976), pp. 484–485.

22. J. M. Oldham, "Inpatient Psychiatry and Milieu," in *Core Readings in Psychiatry:*

An Annotated Guide to the Literature, edited by M. H. Sacks, W. H. Sledge, and P. Rubinton (New York: Praeger, 1984), pp. 341–342.

23. A. M. Kraft, "The Therapeutic Community," in *American Handbook of Psychiatry.* Vol. III, edited by S. Arieti (New York: Basic Books, 1966), pp. 542–551.

24. Main, "The Hospital as a Therapeutic Institution."

25. S. H. Foulkes, *Therapeutic Group Analysis* (New York: Intern. Univ. Press, 1964), p. 215.

26. B. J. Sadock and H. I. Kaplan, "History of Group Psychiatry," in *Comprehensive Group Psychotherapy.* 2nd edt., edited by H. I. Kaplan and B. J. Sadock (Baltimore/London: Williams & Wilkins, 1983, p. 2.

27. A. Myerson, "Theory and Principles of the 'Total Push' Method in the Treatment of Chronic Schizophrenia," *Am. J. Psychiatry* xcv (1939):1197–1204.

28. Sullivan, "Sociopsychiatric Research."

29. F. Fromm-Reichman, *Principles of Intensive Psychotherapy* (Chicago University of Chicago Press, 1950).

30. R. P. Knight and C. R. Friedman, *Psychoanalytic Psychiatry and Psychology: Clinical and Theoretical Papers.* (New York: International Universities, 1970).

31. H. F. Ellenberger, *The Discovery of the Unconscious: The History and Evolution of Dynamic Psychiatry.* (New York: Basic Books, 1970).

32. B. Russell, *A History of Western Philosophy.* (New York: Simon & Schuster, 1972), pp. 675–836.

33. Ellenberger, *The Discovery of the Unconscious,* p. 195.

34. *Ibid.,* p. 197.

35. *Ibid.,* p. 202.

36. *Ibid.,* p. 200.

37. E. Harms, "Modern Psychotherapy—150 Years Ago," *J. Mental Science* CIII (1957):804–809.

38. C. A. Iderer, *Grundriss der Seelenheilkunde,* 2 vols (Berlin: Verlag von T. C. F. Enslin, 1835).

39. H. Neumann, *Lehrbuch der Psychiatrie* (Erlangen: F. Enke, 1859).

40. J. S. Bockoven, *Moral Treatment in Community Mental Health.* (New York: Springer, 1972), p. 69.

41. Ellenberger, *The Discovery of the Unconscious.*

42. *Ibid.,* pp. 218–223.

43. *Ibid.,* p. 284.

44. *Ibid.,* p. 242.

45. T. Meynert, *Klinische Vorlesungen uber Psychiatrie.* (Vienna: Braumuller, 1890).

46. Ellenberger, *The Discovery of the Unconscious.*

47. E. Kraepelin, *Lectures on Clinical Psychiatry.* (Rev. & Ed. by T. Johnstone) (New York: Hafner, 1968).

48. H. C. Burdett, *Hospital and Asylums of the World,* Vol. 1 (London: Churchill, 1891), p. 110.

49. Ellenberger, *The Discovery of the Unconscious,* pp. 534–546.

50. *Ibid.,* p. 231.

51. *Ibid.,* p. 502–504, 541.

52. *Ibid.,* p. 279.

53. J. C. Reil, *Rhapsodien uber die Anwendung der psychischen Cur-Methoden auf Geisteszerruttungen* (Halle: Curt, 1803).

54. M. Eliade, *Mythes, Rêves et Mystéres (Paris: Gallimard, 1957),* pp. 48–59.

55. Sadock & Kaplan, "History of Group Psychiatry."

56. J. H. Pratt, "The Class Method of Treating Consumption in the Homes of the Poor," *J. Am. Med. Assoc.* 49 (1907):755–759.

57. Sadock & Kaplan, "History of Group Psychiatry," p. 1.

58. S. B. Hadden, "A Glimpse of Pioneers in Group Psychotherapy," *Int. J. Group Psychother.* XXV, 4 (1975):371–378.

59. H. Mullen and M. Rosenbaum, *Group Psychotherapy: Theory and Practice,* 2nd. ed (New York: The Free Press, 1978), pp. 5–7.

60. Sadock & Kaplan, "History of Group Psychiatry."

61. E. W. Lazell, "The Group Treatment of Dementia Praecox," *Psychoanal Rev.* 8 (1921):168–179.

62. R. Battegay, "Group Therapy in Switzerland," unpublished paper (December, 1981), 1.

63. E. Bleuler, *Lehrbuch der Psychiatrie.* (Textbook in Psychiatry) Umgearbeitet von M. Blueler, 9th ed (Berlin/Gottingen/Heeidelberg: Springer, 1955).

64. J. E. Straehelin, "Grundsatzliches uber den Ausbau und Betrieb psychiatrischer Spitaler," (Principles of the Construction and Operation of Psychiatric Hospitals). *Schweiz. Arch. Neurol. Neurochir. Psychiatr.* 69 (1952):436.

65. R. Battegay, "Personal communication," May 1985.

66. L. Wender, "The Dynamics of Group Psychotherapy and Its Application," *J. Nerv. Ment. Dis.* 84 (1936):54–60.

67. P. Schilder, "The Analysis of Ideologies as a Psychotherapeutic Method, Especially in Group Treatment," *Am. J. Psychiatry* 93 (1936): 601.

68. W. R. Bion, *Experiences in Groups and Other Papers* (London: Tavistock Publications, 1961).

69. S. H. Foulkes, *Therapeutic Group Analysis* (New York: International Universities Press, 1977).

70. H. Ezriel, "A Psychoanalytic Approach to the Treatment of Patients in Groups," *J. Ment. Sci.* 96 (1950):744–747.

71. T. F. Main, "Some Psychodynamic Aspects of Large Groups," *Archivio di Psicologia, Neurologia e Psichiatria.* 35, 4 (1974):446–452.

72. Foulkes, *Therapeutic Group Analysis.*

73. *Ibid.*, pp. 207–219.

74. *Ibid.*, p. 195.

75. *Ibid.*, pp. 192–193.

76. *Ibid.*, p. 207.

77. A. Friedemann, "Gruppentherapie und Gruppendiagnostik an Kindern," *z. Diagnost. Psychol. Rers. Forsch.* 5 (1957):295–306.

78. R. Battegay, "Group Therapy in Switzerland," unpublished paper, (1983) 2.

79. J. L. Moreno, "Application of the Group Method to Classification", *National Committee on Prisons and Labor, 1932.*

80. R. J. Corsini, "Historic Background of Group Psychotherapy: A Critique," *Group Psychotherapy* 3 (1955):223.

81. J. S. Rutan, "Compassion and Understanding—A Conversation with Max Day," *Group* 8 (1984):39–46.

82. C. T. Standish, J. Curri, E. V. Semrad, and M. Day, "Some Difficulties in Group Psychotherapy with Psychotics," *Am. J. Psychiatr.* 109 (1952):283–286.

83. M. Day and E. V. Semrad, "Group Therapy with Neurotics and Psychotics," in *Comprehensive Group Psychotherapy,* edited by H. I. Kaplan and B. J. Sadock (Baltimore: Williams & Wilkens, 1971), pp. 566–580.

84. M. Day and E. V. Semrad, "Group Therapy with Psychotics—Twenty Years Later," in *Group Psychotherapy and Group Functions, Collected Readings,* rev. ed (New York: Basic Books, 1973), pp. 493–499.

85. Rutan, "Compassion and Understanding."

86. *Ibid.*, p. 40.

87. J. W. Thomas, "Group Psychotherapy: A Review of Recent Literature." *Psychosom. Med.* 5 (1943):166–180.

88. W. C. Hulse, "Curative Elements in Group Psychotherapy," *Topical Problems of Psychotherapy* 5:90–101.

89. M. Rosenbaum, "Group Psychotherapy: Heritage, History and the Current Scene," in *Group Psychotherapy: Theory and Practice,* edited by H. Mullen and M. Rosenbaum (New York: The Free Press, 1978), p. 6.

90. Wender, "The Dynamics of Group Psychotherapy and Its Application."

91. Schilder, "The Analysis of Ideologies as a Psychotherapeutic Method."

92. Foulkes, *Therapeutic Group Analysis.*

93. Bion, *Experiences in Groups and Other Papers.*

94. R. Battegay, Personal Communication, see footnote p. 23.

95. E. Semrad and M. Day, "Group Therapy with Neurotics and Psychotics," in *Group Treatment of Mental Illness,* Vol. six, edited by H. I. Kaplan and B. J. Sadock (New York: Jason Aronson, Inc., 1972), pp. 78–91.

96. R. Dreikurs and R. Corsini, "Twenty Years of Group Psychotherapy: Purposes, Methods and Mechanisms," *Am. J. Psychiatr.* 110 (1954):570–571.

97. *Ibid.*, p. 568.

98. L. C. Marsh, "Group Treatment by the Psychological Equivalent of the Revival," *Ment. Hyg.* 15 (1931):328.

99. Foulkes, *Therapeutic Group Analysis.*

100. R. H. Klein, "Inpatient Group Psychotherapy: Practical Considerations and Special Problems," *Int. J. Group Psychother.* 27 (1977):201–214.

101. H. Kibel, "Inpatient Group Psychotherapy," *Am. J. Psychiatr.* 138 (1981): 65–70.

102. C. A. Rice and J. S. Rutan, "Boundary Maintenance in Inpatient Therapy Groups," *Int. J. Group Psychother.* 31 (1981):297–309.

103. E. C. Lonergan, *Group Intervention: How to Begin and Maintain Groups in Medical and Psychiatric Settings* (New York: Jason Aronson, 1982).

104. I. Yalom, *Inpatient Group Psychotherapy* (New York: Basic Books, 1983).

105. S. Hannah, "Countertransference in Inpatient Group Psychotherapy: Implications for Technique," *Int. J. Group Psychother.* 34 (1984):257–272.

106. J. S. Maxmen, "Helping Patients Survive Theories: The Practice of an Educative Model," *Int. J. Group Psychother.* 34 (1984):355–368.

107. Dreikurs and Corsini, "Twenty Years of Group Psychotherapy."

108. Lazell, "The Group Treatment of Dementia Praecox."

109. Foulkes, *Therapeutic Group Analysis.*

2

Theoretical Basis for Inpatient Group Therapy

All psychotherapists must have a theory to draw on as they work with their patients. Intuition is not only an insufficient guide in doing psychotherapy, it often leads one down the wrong paths. In the first part of this chapter we discuss some of the central concepts of psychodynamic theory on which this book is based, and in the second part we discuss some of the central concepts of systems theory that provide a valuable link between the psychodynamic understandings of our patients and their groups, and the hospitals in which those groups meet.

> CLINICAL VIGNETTE. *A group consisting of six highly impaired inpatients convened for its regular Monday meeting, the first of five weekly meetings. Abby, a highly anxious and often psychotic women was fidgeting endlessly on the couch. She rummaged through her purse, alternately emptying the contents and putting them back. Her behaviors were quite distracting, through no one confronted her about them.*
>
> *Bob was in his typical fetal position at the other end of the couch. Though he had attended the group faithfully for a week, he had not yet spoken or opened his eyes during a meeting.*
>
> *Carol sat in a chair next to the leader, and proceeded to stare at him as the meeting began.*
>
> *Arnie and Betty arrived two minutes late, conspicuously carrying coffee. They continued a conversation they had begun in the coffee shop, talking about Betty's retarded brother who was coming to visit later this afternoon.*

The other members sat quietly as Arnie and Betty spoke. No one seemed particularly interested in their conversation, and no one looked at them.

Betty was saying, "I love my brother. He was the only one in the family who was nice to me. He may have been mentally deficient, but he could love. He still can, though it isn't obvious to anyone but me."

At that point, Abby stood up and stared at Bob, her companion on the couch. She glared at him, though he seemed not to notice. Finally she screamed at the top of her lungs, "LOOK AT ME!" The power of her affect was frightening, and various members cringed. But Bob just opened his eyes and looked up and smiled. Betty began to weep and got up and fled the room, followed closely by Arnie. Abby began to howl, a long, low scream with no words. Carol put her hands over her ears and slid to the floor, where she lay face down and very still.

At this point Arnie returned, pulling Betty back into the group with him, and they sat down and began discussing Betty's brother again, even though Abby continued to scream.

How would you respond if you were the leader of this difficult group? How would you decide what would be the best course of action? Should Abby be removed by attendants and sedated? Should this meeting be prematurely terminated on the basis that things had gotten out of control? Should the leader "teach" these patients the inappropriateness of their behaviors?

This book is based on psychodynamic theory. Psychodynamic theory, in turn, is based on Freud's psychoanalytic theory and the modifications of that theory that have occurred since Freud's time. A hallmark of psychodynamic theory is the conviction that behavior is meaningful and not random. This means that even the most unusual behavior, including that of severely regressed hospitalized patients, serves a valuable function. This approach is antithetical to the "removal of symptoms" philosophy that so often permeates psychiatric hospitals. Although it is true that certain symptoms are too dangerous to the patients and others to be allowed to continue, more often than not we prefer to view the symptoms and discomforts of our patients as communications about underlying problems that must be addressed if they are to be helped. This means clinicians must artfully balance the danger of the symptoms with the need to understand rather than eliminate them.

In the example above, from a dynamic perspective the patients are both demonstrating survival skills and also communicating about their inner worlds by their behaviors. The goals of the group therapist include helping the patients begin to understand both the etiology of their feelings and behaviors and also the effects that those feelings and behaviors have on others. To further elucidate this point, we now give more information about the patients.

Abby was the second of two children. Her older brother was a childhood schizophrenic and spent much of their early years in a catatonic state. This severely disturbed boy was managed at home, and the parents devoted themselves tirelessly to his care. This often meant that Abby received little attention and spent untold hours occupying herself. During that time she developed a fantasy world of make-believe small friends who lived in the little purse her mother had given her. When she was ten her brother was finally institutionalized, where he lived until he died a few months ago. Upon his death, Abby became floridly psychotic and was hospitalized herself.

Bob was a Viet Nam veteran. He had always been troubled, often in difficulty with the law and considered a problem child by his parents and teachers. He had managed to survive until the stresses of Viet Nam, at which time he had a psychotic break while under enemy fire in the rice paddies. He has been in and out of psychiatric hospitals since that time. He rarely speaks to anyone and often lies curled up in corners of various hospital rooms. Nonetheless, he manages to make it to all his hospital appointments.

Carol is diagnosed as borderline. Her mother died when she was five, and she lived with her father until she was 35. At that time her father retired and moved to Florida, leaving Carol to fend for herself in the Northeast. She lived in a small apartment provided by her father and began a series of destructive sexual liaisons with men who beat her, robbed her, and mistreated her in all sorts of ways. In all cases she loved these men passionately and was crushed when they found her neediness overwhelming and left her. On the ward she is very demanding of the male staff members and noncommunicative to the female staff. She rarely speaks to patients.

Arnie is a much higher functioning patient. He worked as an accountant and was hospitalized when he felt overwhelmed by the pressures of his job. This was his first hospitalization and he has used the therapeutic resources well. He has come to understand that his perfectionistic drive has roots in his father's bankruptcy and his own internal wish to save his father by mastering accounting and business procedures.

Betty is also a higher functioning patient. Her hospitalization was the result of her mother's recent death and the resultant responsibility for her ambivalently held retarded brother. Betty felt enormous guilt over her rage that now she was responsible for her brother, and her inability to accept that rage led to her breakdown.

With this background information at his disposal, the therapist was able to review the process of this group and generate some hypotheses about what had occurred. He noted, for example, that Abby was busily going through her purse, and he guessed that this represented a delusional involvement with her imaginary friends – a sure sign of high anxiety. Abby routinely turned to these "friends" when she felt in need of soothing or reassurance.

He noted that Carol looked at him longingly, though this was her usual state and did not indicate anything unusual. Bob's fetal position, likewise, was a normal position for him. Arnie and Betty were linked, and they often managed to arrive late at the group. The leader judged that they were frightened by the irrational behavior so evident in the other members. Their conspicuous coffee cups were clear indication that they had taken group time to purchase coffee rather than to arrive on time. It also was clear that Betty was trying to resolve her complex feelings about her brother, as that was the content of her discussion with Arnie.

The leader recognized that the discussion of Betty's brother directly preceded Abby's yelling at Bob. This led to the hypothesis that Abby had been reminded of her own brother, whose death had been the pre- cipitant for her hospitalization. Furthermore, Bob's silence in the group probably was reminiscent of her brother's catatonia. In this light Abby's outburst at Bob made more sense – she was demanding some recognition as she must have done from her brother. Hearing Betty speaking of her love for a defective brother may have stirred deep feeling in Abby. Bob, responding to that, smiled because in his own primitive way he under- stood that her communication was inviting and not hostile. Betty, seeing the contact between Bob and Abby wept and fled, overwhelmed by her own feelings for her brother.

With this information, and with the psychodynamic conviction that even the most bizarre behaviors are meaningful, the therapist said simply, "Bob's silence and anguish seems to stir deep feelings in many people."

It turned out that this explanation was correct, and Abby sat down and said, "I don't want to talk about my brother!" Betty quickly asso- ciated to her brother and commented that she worried about being able to adequately care for him. She turned to Bob and asked if he felt she could take care of her brother, and Bob, speaking his first words in the group, said, "You're a kind person." The remainder of the meeting was spent in fruitful discussion with all members talking about their families, telling Bob the impact his silence had had on everyone, and connecting with each other again.

Not all interventions have such a dramatic impact, but this example demonstrates how a dynamic therapist can help inpatients learn from their group interactions.

RELEVANT PSYCHODYNAMIC CONCEPTS

There are several fine texts available for readers who need more basic information about psychodynamic principles.[1,2] For our purposes, we will explore a few of the psychodynamic concepts that have most relevance for inpatient group therapists.

TRANSFERENCE

Transference, or the distorting of present-day relationships on the basis of early, formative relationships, became one of Freud's primary tools in helping his patients learn more about their early lives and their inner worlds. It also became the fundamental premise upon which psychoanalytic theory was based. Through careful analysis of the attributes that patients placed on them, analysts were able to deduce much about the nature of those patients' early relationships.

The concept of transference really has to do with the perception of reality. In this regard, Freud's interest is in line with an important philosophical inquiry that long preceded him. The notion that "what you see is not what you get" has legitimate scholarly antecedents. Plato[3] told the story of Socrates meeting and questioning Theaetetus, a sixteen-year-old boy renowned in his village for his wisdom. The seventy-year-old Socrates asks, "What is knowledge," and the boy responds, "Knowledge is perception."

Socrates, in his famous questioning method, draws out the full implications of the boy's position. Reality is appearance, "What *seems* or *appears* to me *is* to me."

Freud noted that his patients often had incorrect perceptions of him, and that they lived "as if" their perceptions were true. He first mentioned the concept of transference in his *Studies on Hysteria* in 1895.[4]

The importance of this concept for inpatient therapists is the recognition that group members will often attribute qualities to them that belong to significant people in their lives and do not necessarily fit the therapists themselves. Several consequences follow from this. First, it can be helpful for therapists to realize that many of the qualities, both good and bad, that group members attribute to them are directed at whom they represent and not at them personally. This can often make it easier for therapists to bear moments of high discomfort.* Second, and more importantly, the qualities attributed to the therapists will give them some understanding of their patients and their struggles. If certain patients view their therapists, no matter how benign they may be, with unremitting fear and feel unable to speak in their groups, it gives the therapists an important "window" into the nature of their earlier relationships and their current inner world. It is important to add that patients also will develop transference relationships with their peer group members. In our vignette, most of the members reacted to Bob's silence through the prisms of earlier relationships. Betty experienced Bob in the light of her relationship with her brother whose love was present but not obvious, whereas Abby viewed him in terms of her brother who got most of the attention in the family. The nature of those earlier relationships led them to react to Bob in contrasting ways. One of the primary advantages of group therapy is that the members can develop a variety of transference relationships, thus allowing therapists to view the inner and interpersonal worlds of their patients through a number of different "windows."[5]

Sometimes, the distortions created by a patient's transference can be so great that he or she may be unable to distinguish the relationship with the therapist from the original relationship on which the transference is based. A patient may then not only relate to the therapist as though she was his mother, he may believe that she is his mother. This is called a psychotic transference and sometimes is evident in an inpatient group. Most transferences are not psychotic, but members of inpatient groups typically have greater difficulty distinguishing the real therapists from their distorted pictures of them than do members of outpatient groups.

Defenses

All organisms must find ways to protect themselves against threats from the outside world. Some animals do it by changing the color of their skin to match the surrounding environment, and people do it by

---

*This should not preclude therapists from being alert to those occasions when their behavior may engender the comments they receive from group members, whether pleasant or unpleasant.

forming groups, building secure homes, and so on. Without that protection organisms and people could not survive.

People, as psychological beings, also need to protect themselves from the fears and anxieties that arise when they feel threatened by the loss of sustaining relationships, or overwhelmed by a sense of disorganization or paralyzed by seemingly unresolvable conflicts. In psychodynamic theory that protection is provided by the defenses. For example, if a very austere individual begins to experience strong sexual or aggressive impulses that run counter to his strict ethical convictions, he may become highly conflicted and anxious. If the anxiety becomes intolerable and threatens his capacity to function, his psychological protective mechanism may banish the impulse from his awareness, that is, repress it. Now the individual has no active awareness of the impulses, though they may find expression in some behavior, such as an increased vehemence against the "evils of sex." Without defenses, such as repression, people could not survive as viable, autonomously functioning persons.[6–11]

There are many ways that people defend themselves against unnecessary anxiety. For example, among the defenses delineated by Anna Freud,[12] were regression, repression, reaction formation, isolation, undoing, projection, denial, and sublimation. Her list does not exhaust the possible ways in which individuals may defend themselves. Indeed, almost any kind of behavior may serve defensive purposes. Anna Freud noted the complexity and variability of defenses when she pointed out that behavior, such as excessive aggression, which would normally seem reprehensible, may in fact be a defense. For example, the young boy who bullies other children may be defending himself against overwhelming fears of his father or mother by identifying with them.

The defenses are also hierarchically related. That is, some defenses are more complex and sophisticated than others and usually come into being at a later developmental stage in individuals' lives. Rationalization, for instance, is a more complex defense than denial. Rationalization is the very common tendency of people to interpret their behavior in such a way as to make it seem reasonable, even when it is not. A man who fails to show up for an important appointment, for example, may excuse himself by saying, "I was so busy at the office, I simply forgot." Such a defense is possible only when the individuals have developed the capacity to think in terms of cause and effect and the ability to conceptualize complex relationships. Denial, on the other hand, stems from that stage of development when, as a young child, one can change or block out reality simply by saying so. Often children will say, "Let's pretend it didn't happen." And, indeed, they will then continue their activity as if the event in question had never occurred. Usually, denial is used by adults with severe pathology or under extreme stress. On the other hand, those of us who have lost our car keys just before driving to a dental appointment cannot deny the active involvement of the unconscious in protecting us from anxious or painful situations.

People use many defenses, not just one. In most people, however, certain kinds of defenses predominate.

The defenses of patients we meet in inpatient groups are usually found low on the hierarchy. Among the most common are denial, projection, and severe acting out. Acting out means reducing anxiety from internal distress by a piece of behavior, such as leaving the room. In our opening illustration, Betty sought to reduce the distress she experienced by leaving the group. Through projection, people defend themselves by placing their fears onto someone or something else. Thus, an individual, anxious and conflicted about homosexual wishes, may accuse another person of being homosexual.

Although defenses are necessary, they can also be problematic. Sometimes defenses create the very thing we fear. The patient who defends himself by remaining aloof from others, also risks losing the relationships he needs to sustain himself. The defenses of our patients are often problematic in this manner.

It is not, however, the goal of psychodynamic therapists to break through those defenses; after all it is those defenses that have enabled the patients to survive. Rather their goal, where possible, is to help them understand the fears and the conflicts that make those defenses necessary so that they can substitute more effective ones. When the therapist made clear the source of the members' anxiety in our illustration, Betty did not need to leave the group again, but rather could talk about the nature of her concerns without feeling overwhelmed by them.

There are times, however, when it is necessary to reduce the external source of the patient's anxiety before the defenses can be modified and understanding begin. This happens when a therapist sits with a frightened schizophrenic patient, neither intruding upon the patient nor leaving him, but actively maintaining the relationship until the patient feels safe enough to speak.[13]

In the next section, we address two other defenses that play a central role in the lives of our patients. Because of their complexity and importance, we examine their roots in more detail than the defenses.

OBJECT RELATIONS, SPLITTING, AND PROJECTIVE IDENTIFICATION

Object Relations. The role of relationships in people's lives has always been an important aspect of psychoanalytic theory. One of the first psychodynamic theorists to pay special attention to that role was Harry Stack Sullivan. He recognized the importance of relationships not only in significantly contributing to who we are, but also in healing us. Along with Frieda Fromm-Reichmann he worked very successfully with schizophrenic patients. In treating these patients Sullivan and Fromm-Reichmann encouraged the patients to build a relationship with them, and then they acted as bridges between the patients and the outside world.[14-16]

Other psychodynamic therapists who place particular emphasis on the role of relationships are the object relations theorists, such as Klein,[17] Balint,[18] Winnicott,[19] Fairbairn,[20] and Mahler.[21] Object relations theorists, in agreement with Sullivan, argue that from the earliest moments of life an infant seeks to make and maintain attachments with persons in the immediate environment, usually the mother. If the initial attachments are successful, they gradually broaden to include more and more people.[22]

In addition, they pay special attention to how those early relationships become internalized by the infant until the infant develops a cohesive sense of self that is distinct from, but in relationship with, others.[23]

Many of the patients we see in inpatient groups have had biological or interpersonal environments, or both, that have led to less than adequate attachments. Some have had attachments that were tenuous at best, others have made attachments that were engulfing and prevented adequate differentiation of themselves from others, and others have had attachments that were unpredictable; one moment close and warm, the next cold and distant. Often, as a result, their sense of self is not well defined, or if defined, readily subject to disintegration when they are under stress.

A number of mechanisms make possible the internalization of infants' relationships with their mothers and other family members and the development of cohesive selves. Two of these mechanisms play a significant role in inpatient groups: splitting and projective identification.

Splitting. Splitting[24] is a precursor or simple form of differentiation, and as such is an essential process in managing life. It is also a defense. In internalizing their early relationships, infants use splitting in both those senses.

During the first few months of life there is little distinction between infants and their mothers, and their inner models of those early relationships reflect that oneness. Those models are called self-object images, acknowledging the fact that infants develop images of themselves and their mothers that are initially indistinguishable from one another. After the first few months infants gradually develop distinct images of their mothers and of themselves, but at first cannot conceive of one without the other.

Under optimal circumstances, infants experience the early months of life as generally pleasant and satisfying, which again is reflected in their images, called *good* self-object images. The unpleasant experiences of those early months and the aggressively toned responses to those experiences are reflected in the development of a separate set of images called *bad* self-object images. Thus the good and bad experiences are split from each other even though the sources of those experiences may be the same.

The process of splitting continues apace as infants begin to separate from their mothers. Moving from a symbiotic, undifferentiated relationship to a differentiated one in which infants can experience themselves as separate from their mothers is both desirable and rewarding, and is reflected in increasingly separate self and object images. But separation can also lead to considerable frustration, anxiety, and distress for infants. Infants' needs are not gratified instantly, mother is not always present, and feeling separate from her can be frightening. On occasion infants respond to those frustrations and fears with outbursts of rage. This further highlights an ongoing problem for infants. The problem is, how does one deal with a good mother who causes bad things to happen? Infants solve the problem by splitting their experience of the mother into its component parts and viewing the mother who does good things and the mother who does bad things as different persons. This enables them to keep the all-good mother intact and deny the existence of the bad one. Infants do the same thing with their own aggressive and unpleasant experiences. Their internal images then become a good self-image, a bad self-image, a good object-image, and a bad object-image. As they mature, infants integrate those images and relationships until they are able to experience themselves and others as whole people with both "good" and "bad" components. At that time their sense of themselves and others as distinct, cohesive, and related individuals becomes established.

Thus, through splitting, infants break down their interpersonal experiences, the associated physiological and emotional responses, and the inner objects into their component parts to differentiate from those around them. In addition, by splitting bad experiences from good experiences, and bad objects from good objects they are better able to handle the anxiety and distress generated by differentiating. Both aspects of splitting enable infants to learn, grow, and mature. As Hanna Segal wrote:

> It is splitting which allows the ego to emerge out of chaos and to order its experiences. This ordering of experience which occurs with the process of splitting into a good and bad object, however excessive and extreme it may be to begin with, nevertheless orders the universe of the child's emotional and sensory impressions and is a precondition of later integration. It is the basis of what is later to become the faculty of discrimination. . . .[25]

Splitting only becomes a problem in infant development if it fails to take place or if it becomes rigidly entrenched so that integration cannot take place. If it fails to take place, the infant will remain undifferentiated and may become psychotic and unable to effectively distinguish the inner from the outer world and him or herself from others. If it becomes rigidly entrenched, the infant may become an adult with borderline psychopathology, in which the world becomes severely split into good and bad people, good and bad self, and good and bad experiences.

Splitting is commonly seen in inpatient groups as a way of coping. It is not uncommon to find inpatients whose inner objects are firmly divided into "good" and "bad," and whose relationships reflect that inner split. In our vignette, Betty readily divided the staff into good and bad objects. Male staff were good "mothers" from whom she expected and demanded a lot, and to whom she often related intensely. Female staff were bad "mothers" from whom she expected little and from whom she remained aloof.

Projective Identification.   Projective identification[26-28] is closely related to splitting and occurs in the earliest stages of development when the boundaries between infants and their mothers are most permeable. When infants become enraged and anxious during these early stages mothers usually become instantly aware of it. Their infants' discomforts seem to be part of themselves and they feel compelled to do something about them. Ideally, they respond in a calming and uncritical manner, which more often than not calms the infants.

Viewed from the infants' perspectives, the process may be described thus: because of the discomfort created by their rage and anxiety, they seek to get rid of those unpleasant feelings by splitting them off from themselves and projecting them into their mothers. The infants become calm as they take back into themselves the rage and anxiety in their mothers along with their calming responses to them. This process is called reintrojection. In time, the infants become able to calm themselves as a consequence of having reintrojected these and other calming experiences.

As with splitting, projective identification serves both learning and defensive functions. By projecting into their mothers the infants learn how to tolerate discomfort and how to comfort themselves. It also serves a defensive purpose by protecting infants from unnecessary discomfort until they are more able to manage it themselves.

Projective identification becomes a problem for infants if the mothers do not respond to their projections adequately. This can occur because of the mothers' personality deficiencies, external circumstances, deficiencies in the infants' innate capacities, or all of the above. If mothers respond in kind to their infants' projections of rage and anxiety, or fail to respond, the reintrojected contents become increasingly discomforting rather than comforting. Under these circumstances infants become unable to learn effective ways to comfort themselves or to defend themselves more effectively against distress. As a result, most future relationships for such unfortunate infants will be highly colored by attempts to manipulate others into containing unpleasant affects. In the most extreme cases individuals seek, through projection, to remove themselves from the capacity to experience, as in certain forms of schizophrenia.[29]

Inpatient group therapists frequently experience the impact of projective identification from group members or other patients on the unit. On those occasions they feel or behave in ways that are *not* consistent with their usual ways of feeling or behaving. They may be surprised by the intensity of their anger at, or by their sadistic manner toward certain patients when there seem to be no obvious reasons for feeling or behaving in that manner. They feel they are playing a part in someone else's fantasy.[30]

Bob's role in our opening vignette may now be viewed a little more fully. Despite remaining quiet in the group, he had a profound and often troubling impact on the therapist and the group members. Prior to this session, the therapist had been aware of feeling drained and enraged as he watched Bob or attempted to speak to him. He was puzzled about why he felt that way, was uncomfortable about it, and as often as not was happy just to let Bob be. He recalled how secretly relieved he had been when Bob was late for group on one occasion and how the group become somber and sluggish after he finally arrived.

When Abby yelled "Look at me!" the therapist felt some relief, and thought "God, I've wanted to yell at Bob too, 'Stop draining me!' " Carol looked like she had been drained. As the therapist reviewed all that had happened in this session, he realized also how Bob, though quiet, had been communicating to him and all the members in a variety of nonverbal ways that seemed to bypass their normal cognitive processes. The members and the leader had become the containers of Bob's seemingly limitless dependency and rage, and they felt drained and angered by it. They also became the containers of his fear of being drained by others. For his part, Bob had split off these unwanted parts of himself and identified with them in the members as they lived out his fantasies.

As the members talked afterward about the impact of his silence on them, Bob's anger and dependency became less frightening to him and to the others.

Under optimal circumstances projective identification matures into the capacity for "vicarious introspection and, in its most sublimated form, for empathy."[31] That is, adults become able to project themselves into others and identify with them without seeking to change them.

INTERPRETATION

After examining the transferences, defenses, and object relationships of their patients, and drawing tentative hypotheses about their meanings, the question then is, "How is this information made available to the patients?" Interpretation is the major means by which therapists attempt to make the information available to patients to help them begin to understand their out of awareness feelings, thoughts, and behaviors.

In classical psychoanalysis this was the main vehicle of change. The therapist was the expert who "understood" and who offered the fruits of his or her understanding through interpretations. Though much of what occurred in psychoanalysis was quite emotional and seemingly irrational or unreasonable, interpretation was viewed as using reason, or one's cognitive resources, to make those emotions and related behaviors understandable and therefore give the patient mastery over them. Thus, if a patient was consistently late for his sessions, felt very uneasy, and described dreams of doing harm to people in authority, the therapist might explain that he is uneasy because he is angry at her and expresses it by being late. Depending on what additional data the patient shared, the therapist might also suggest that the patient's way of handling his anger was a pattern he developed earlier to cope with his fear of a particular parent. The therapist does this with the intention of enabling the patient to express his current feelings directly, and of helping him understand the roots of his emotionally laden assumption (the transference) that has now come to light, namely that it is dangerous to express anger directly to persons in authority.

Modern psychoanalytic theory relies much more heavily on the relationship between the therapist and the patient for both understanding and change. This has particular significance for hospital groups. Inpatients often have limited cognitive ability, so their capacity to use the cognitive aspects of psychodynamic therapy is often inhibited. Thus, we are forced to rely much more fully on the relationship that our patients establish with us and with their peers as the means to gain understanding and effect change. In a group the therapist may behave in ways that clearly indicate that the patient is understood without demanding any further exploration. For example, a therapist may postpone a patient's admission into a group because he recognizes that the patient's fear of the group is overwhelming, or he may set limits on another patient because he recognizes that she needs support to contain her behavior.

Clarifying interpretations[32] are generally the most effective interpretations in inpatient groups. These interpretations are statements that seek to bring understanding to patients' behaviors and experiences by linking them to current or recent precipitating events. Thus a therapist might say that the group members are angry and depressed because he missed the last two sessions. The intervention made by the therapist in our opening illustration, "Bob's silence and anguish seems to stir deep feelings in many people" was also a clarifying interpretation. Interpretations of this nature give meaning to the patients' behavior, enable them to talk about it and increase their mastery of it. They do not seek to uncover the historic roots of the patients' behavior. Besides their cognitive limitations, the members are often too caught up in the crisis of their illness to respond favorably to such self-exploration, that understanding usually comes later in outpatient treatment. There are some patients, however, particularly those whose "breakdown" was largely in reaction to a crisis, who can benefit from interpretations that connect past and present experiences.

SYSTEMS THEORY

The concepts we discussed so far have focused primarily on the individual group patient. Attention also has been paid to the relationships between patients, and between patients and therapists in the examination of such concepts as transference, splitting, and projective identification. Attention, however, needs to be given to concepts that are more directly applicable to the groups themselves and to the hospitals or hospital units in which those groups meet. It will also be particularly advantageous if those concepts can provide bridges between the individual, the group, and the unit. With those goals in mind we turn to the work of the systems theorists who are among the forerunners in these areas.

Systems theorists note that our universe is neither "completely homogeneous nor totally discrepant."[33] Rather it is made up of many, relatively distinct parts, that they refer to as *systems,* and among which a variety of relationships may be observed. That is, the universe has a *structure*; the parts or systems can be organized in various ways. Those structures, however, are not static but change over time. Some parts, such as a gas, change very rapidly, whereas others, such as a land mass, change very slowly over long periods of time. In the words of Robin Skinner, "The universe not only has structure, but seen over time is a *process*, a changing structure where the changes also show relationships one to another."[34]

What is true of the universe as a whole is true of the parts or systems that compose it. They are composed of other smaller parts or systems among which a variety of relationships may be observed: they have structures. And, like the universe, they are processes, they change over time, and those changes show relationships one to another. Systems have many forms, from the concrete to the abstract. An island is a system, and so is psychodynamic theory. It is a system of thought. Thus, an inpatient group is a system and is part of a larger system, the inpatient unit.

Systems theorists attempt to describe and understand the relationships among and within whole systems, that is, their structure and their process. It is not surprising that they define a system as a set of elements in dynamic interaction.[35] This is an apt description of the interacting members who make up a group. A number of concepts that systems theorists have developed – boundary, hierarchy, isomorphism, and steady state – are particularly helpful in understanding and leading inpatient groups, and in developing an inpatient group therapy program. Consistent with a systems perspective, all these concepts are closely interrelated.

BOUNDARIES

A boundary refers to that part of a system that separates it from its environment or from other systems, such as the skin around our bodies or the banks of a river. A boundary determines what enters or leaves a system and what does *not* enter or leave. In an inpatient group the boundary determines who is in the group and who is not, who enters and leaves, as well as when they enter and leave, and it determines what information stays in the group and what information may leave the group.

Some boundaries permit nothing to enter or leave a system. These are referred to as closed systems, which usually remain unaffected by their environment and do not change. There is probably no such thing as a completely closed system, but some come quite close, such as aluminum, which is little affected by its environment. By contrast, other boundaries allow so much to enter or leave the system that there is little distinction between the system and its environment. In time the system ceases to exist because it becomes indistinguishable from its environment. This is seen in certain gases, and can be seen in an inpatient group when the boundaries are not well maintained.

> EXAMPLE. *At a workshop on inpatient groups, a therapist described how difficult it had become for her to maintain her groups. Patients frequently missed sessions despite her best efforts. It was rare to have a well-filled group, and some of her groups simply died. Discussion revealed that if the psychiatrists who were treating her group members came into the hospital when her group was meeting, invariably, they took the patients out of the group for their individual sessions. Such a failure of boundary maintenance by the hospital and the therapist led to the demise of some of the groups and seriously threatened the life of others.*

Living systems are systems whose boundaries are permeable enough (open enough) to permit exchange with their environment so that they may be renewed and grow and change, but closed enough so that they can maintain a distinction between themselves and their environment. Boundaries are also dynamic. The degree of openness and closedness varies. A system may be open to a particular exchange with its environment at a particular time and closed to the same exchange at another time. A mother and father (the parental system), for instance, may be available to meet and play with their children at one time, but later, when they wish to make love, they will exclude them. Some systems theorists,[36] in an attempt to convey the dynamic quality of boundaries. have suggested that we use the verb boundarying rather than the noun boundary, because the latter suggests a static, unchanging quality.

HIERARCHY

Hierarchy refers to the fact that a system is usually part of another larger and more complex system referred to as a suprasystem, and at the same time is made up of a number of smaller and less complex systems called subsystems. An inpatient group, for instance, is part of the larger, more complex hospital and is itself made up of a number of separate individuals.

ISOMORPHISM

Isomorphism, which literally means having the same form, refers to the fact that although each living system has unique characteristics, it shares basic organizational characteristics with other living systems. This is particularly true of systems that are closely related. Isomorphism is of particular importance and value when seeking to understand the dynamics of an inpatient group or hospital unit. It means, for instance, that the nature of the hospital organization will be paralleled in the organization and behavior of the group and of the individual members of that group. The same holds true for the hospital staff. That is, the organization of the hospital system is paralleled in the subsystems contained within it.

> EXAMPLE. *An inpatient group therapist could not understand why she was having so much difficulty leading her group. The members were alternately quiet and despairing, and aggressive and belligerent. None of her interventions made any impact; she felt at a loss. After some questions from a consultant she recalled an event she had "forgotten." The previous week a patient had killed himself while on a weekend pass. The staff were shocked by this event, but decided to go about their work as usual. The event was subsequently "forgotten" by the group therapist and the rest of the staff. Except, that doing "work as usual" did not seem possible*

for the therapist or her group. Following the consultation, the therapist returned to her group and, at an opportune moment, raised the question of the suicide and its impact on the members. The mood of the group changed and all the members talked eagerly, if uncomfortably, about the suicide, their fears of doing the same thing, and the safety of the hospital or the lack of it. Later, the staff also talked productively about the event.

That event not only illustrated isomorphism, but also reinforced, in a social setting, what Freud had observed with individuals. That which is excluded from awareness will find expression in some other way. In this instance, the "forgotten" event sought experession through the behavior of the group members. In addition, that "forgotten" event and its expression in the group members demonstrates the isomorphism between individual systems and social systems.

The process may also work in reverse. That is, the internal organization of a patient's object relations will, at times, be paralleled in that person's relations with members of the group and with members of the staff. For instance, on psychiatric units it is well known that a patient whose inner object relations are rigidly divided into bad and good objects will frequently divide staff members into two opposing camps, those supporting the patient's behavior and those opposing it. Such a patient may divide the therapy group in a similar manner. The concept of projective identification that we discussed earlier suggests how that process may come into being.

STEADY STATE

A steady state is a characteristic of a living system, and refers to the system's capacity to change gradually over time as the result of taking in information, and matter–energy from its environment, while at the same time maintaining a consistent and stable internal organization. In addition, that change is usually a change from a relatively simple organization to a more complex and multilayered one. This is seen in the growth of the human body. It remains organizationally stable from day to day making it possible for those who know us to recognize us after an absence, yet, it is also constantly changing. As it grows from the body of an infant to that of an adult, it becomes increasingly complex. This is even more true of the human personality as demonstrated in the work of Gordon Allport.[37] It can also be seen in the life of a small company that gradually changes, over many years, to become a multinational corporation. The same characteristic is true of an inpatient therapy group, despite the rate of patient turnover. Although the high rate of patient turnover may make the maintenance of a steady state more difficult, it nevertheless is possible, particularly if the group boundaries are well managed. An inpatient group will carry forward traditions and new learning from generation to generation of inpatients so that an inpatient group that has been existing for four years will have more complex communication, interactive and symbolic systems than one that has just recently begun. That increased complexity of organization makes the group a better "container" for its members than it was during its early stages.

In an attempt to capture this dynamic, self-sustaining quality of living systems, Durkin[38] has suggested that we speak of autonomous living structures rather than systems. The value of Durkin's concept for the inpatient group therapist is that it recognizes the group's capacity for self-sustaining growth, organization, and maintenance.

A corrective needs to be added that allows us to take into consideration the particular difficulties in applying the concept of steady state to inpatient groups. Closed systems or systems whose boundaries are too permeable cannot maintain a steady state. As we noted earlier, closed systems are largely unaffected by their environment and do not grow and change. Any environmental influence is usually quickly counteracted so that the status quo may be maintained: that is, they are homeostatic. On the other hand, a system whose boundaries are too open is excessively heterostatic, that is, it exchanges material between itself and its environment and within itself so rapidly that its very existence becomes threatened. A viable living system, in creating a steady state, manages to strike a balance between those extremes that is sufficiently off center to permit growth and change. In mental illness, personal systems tend to be excessively closed, which results in internal disorganization or a regression from a more complex organization to a simpler one. In patients with severe pathology, such as psychosis, the closedness toward others is particularly severe. Hence, developing a group for psychotic patients that has a reasonable degree of openness and steady state organization can be very difficult. Our experience, however, indicates that it is possible to build such a group. It is, however, important that the therapists be willing to adjust their goals to the limits set by the patients' "closedness."

With this theoretical material as a base, we examine the dynamics of the inpatient therapy group in the next chapter.

REFERENCES

1. C. Brenner, *An Elementary Textbook of Psychoanalysis* (New York: International Univ. Press, 1973).

2. R. F. Sterba, *Introduction to the Psychoanalytic Theory of the Libido* (New York: Robert Brunner, Inc., 1968).

3. *Theaetetus*, (427–347 BC)

4. Freud, (1895) *Studies on Hysteria*. Std. Ed., 12: 123 (London: Hogarth Press, 1956).

5. L. Ormont and H. Stean, *The Practice of Conjoint Therapy: Combining Individual and Group Treatment* (New York: Human Services Press, 1978), pp. 33–38.

6. R. L. Munroe, *Schools of Psychoanalytic Thought* (New York: Holt, Rinehart and Winston, 1955), p. 86.

7. H. Hartman, "Ego Development and the Problem of Adaptation," in The *Organization and Pathology of Thought*, edited by D. Rapaport (New York: International Universities Press, 1958).

8. D. Rapaport, *The Organization and Pathology of Thought* (New York: Columbia University, 1951).

9. E. H. Erikson, *Childhood and Society*, 2nd ed (New York: Norton, 1963).

10. E. Kris, "On Preconscious Mental Processes," in *Organization and Pathology of Thought*, edited by D. Rapaport (New York: International Universities Press, 1958).

11. R. M. Lowenstein, *Drives, Affects and Behaviors* (New York: International Universities Press, 1953).

12. A. Freud, *The Ego and the Mechanisms of Defense* (New York: W. W. Norton, 1945).

13. B. P. Karon and G. R. Vandenbos, *Psychotherapy of Schizophrenia: The Treatment of Choice* (New York: Jason Aronson, 1981), pp. 135–147.

14. H. S. Sullivan, "The Interpersonal Theory of Psychiatry," in *The Collected Works of Harry Stack Sullivan, M.D.* Vol. I, edited by H. S. Perry and M. L. Gawel (New York: W. W. Norton & Co. Inc., 1953), pp. 3–328.

15. Sullivan, "Conceptions of Modern Psychiatry," in *The Collected Works of Harry Stack Sullivan*.

16. B. P. Karon and G. R. Vandenbos, *Psychotherapy of Schizophrenia: The Treatment of Choice* (New York: Jason Aronson, 1981), pp. 19–24.

17. M. Klein, *Contributions to Psycho-analysis: 1921–1945* (New York: Anglobooks, 1952).

18. M. Balint, *Primary Love and Psychoanalytic Technique* (New York: Liveright, 1965).

19. M. Davis and D. Wallbridge, *Boundary and Space: An Introduction to the D. W. Winnicott* (New York: Brunner/Mazel, 1981).

20. W. R. D. Fairbairn, *Object-Relations Theory of Personality* (New York: Basic Books, 1954).

21. M. S. Mahler, *The Selected Papers of Margaret S. Mahler*, Vols I & II (New York: Jason Aronson, 1979).

22. J. Bowlby, *Attachment and Loss*, Vol. I, *Attachment* (New York: Basic Books, 1969). pp. 303–309.

23. O. Kernberg, *Object Relations Theory and Clinical Psychoanalysis* (New York: Jason Aronson, 1976).

24. J. S. Grotstein, *Splitting and Projective Identification* (New York: Jason Aronson, 1981).

25. H. Segal, *Introduction to the Work of Melanie Klein* (New York: Basic Books, 1964), p. 35.

26. L. Horwitz, "Projective Identification in Dyads and Groups," *Int. J. Group Psychother.* 33 (1983):259–279.

27. T. H. Ogden, *Projective Identification and Psychotherapeutic Technique* (New York: Jason Aronson, 1982).

28. Grotstein, *Splitting and Projective Identification*.

29. T. H. Ogden, *Projective Identification and Psychotherapeutic Technique* (New York: Jason Aronson, 1982), pp. 145–150.

30. W. R. Bion, *Experiences in Groups* (New York: Basic Books, 1959), p. 149.

31. J. S. Grotstein, *Splitting and Projective Identification*.

32. H. D. Kibel, "The Rationale for the Use of Group Psychotherapy for Borderline Patients on a Short-Term Unit," *Int. J. Group Psychother.* 38 (1978):339–358.

33. A. C. R. Skinner, *Systems of Family and Marital Psychotherapy* (New York: Brunner/Mazel, 1976), pp. 3–25.

34. *Ibid.*, p. 4.

35. L. von Bertalanffy, *General Systems Theory: Foundations Development, Applications.* rev. ed (New York: Georger Braziller, 1968), pp. 19, 38, 55–56, 83–84.

36. J. E. Durkin, "Foundations of Autonomous Living Structures," in *Living Groups: Group Psychotherapy and General Systems Theory*, edited by J. E. Durkin (New York: Brunner/Mazel, 1981), pp. 33–40.

37. G. W. Allport, *Personality: A Psychological Interpretation* (New York: Holt, 1937).

38. J. E. Durkin, "Foundations of Autonomous Living Structures," *op. cit.*, pp. 24–33.

3

Dynamics of Inpatient Groups

Any group therapist is faced with a bewildering amount of data when leading a group. Different individuals are speaking and behaving, interactions are occurring between subgroups, and the group itself has a certain life and developmental sequence. For the inexperienced group therapist, in particular, that data may sound like a modern day tower of Babel in which nothing makes sense and no one seems to know quite what anyone else is saying. Inpatient therapy groups often seem all the more confusing because of the primitive nature of the material that emerges, augmented by the lack of continuity of membership. This diversity of data, although at times confusing and difficult to organize, is also the source of unique therapeutic power. What seems to be unrelated and extraneous data is usually highly relevant material, rich with diagnostic and therapeutic meaning. The theory presented in the previous chapter will become the road map that will help the therapist follow the workings of the group.

Part of the difficulty in comprehending the data generated by therapy groups is that the therapist must continually confront and understand three distinct but interrelated perspectives: (1) the individual group members, (2) the interactions among the group members, and (3) the workings of the group-as-a-whole.[1] For many therapists this means a major shift from the individual perspective in which they have been trained.

A fundamental assumption, which psychodynamic group therapists make, is that the behaviors we observe in groups are not random and are not newly created just for this situation. Rather, the members use previously adopted measures to cope with the internal and external stresses that presently confront them. In hospital settings, it is usually preferable to understand the responses primarily in relation to the external pressures our patients experience. That is, hospitalized patients have experienced some sort of life crisis, and their hospitalization itself becomes yet another highly significant stimulus to which they are responding. In addition, group therapists must view the communications and behavior of the group and its members in terms of their adaptive tasks.[2] A group and its members are faced with an adaptive task when changes, positive or negative, take place in their internal or external environment. Some of those internal or external changes may be coped with in relative ease, whereas others may lead to increased stress and regression. In this chapter we focus on the adaptive tasks generated by external stress.

THE GROUP MEMBERS

Fundamental to all groups are the individuals who comprise them. Rarely does a *group* come to us for treatment. Rather, individuals come in distress and we choose, on occasion, to treat them in groups. When using the power that groups and group process provide, it behooves the group therapist to remember that it is the individual patient whom we attempt to help.

Individuals who are members of inpatient groups are usually individuals who have significant pathology. That is, they are people for whom the very early experiences of life have been harsh, or who have suffered overwhelming acute crises. Many factors can contribute to psychopathology, but three major ones stand out. For some patients their biological deficits give them limited resources, and they find it difficult to cope with the demands placed on them by their environment, however nourishing or benign. This is probably the case with autistic children and childhood schizophrenics. For others, their families, although encouraging certain aspects of development, severely limited others. This is probably the case with the severe character pathologies, such as borderline patients. Finally, there are patients for whom a specific correlation of environmental factors, along with biological givens, lead to a heightened vulnerability to the assaults that life entails. These individuals include numbers of schizophrenics or severely depressed patients.[3]

Psychodynamic therapy focuses on the environmental and interpersonal viscissitudes of life and their contribution to the intrapsychic problems our patients bear. Though not discounting the potential impact of biological origins of mental illness, the emphasis is on the importance of significant others in the development of personality.

Members of an inpatient therapy group must cope with a number of predictable and interrelated adaptive tasks. They include adapting to the experience of having a ''nervous breakdown,'' of being hospitalized, of living in a community of staff and patients, of coping with staff changes, of being separated from one's family and from one's major occupations in life. Within the group itself, they include making contact with peer members, developing a sense of trust and safety, monitoring one's personal boundaries among a group of others, bearing one's internal discomfort in the face of these other tasks, saying good-bye to other patients who leave, and finally saying good-bye to the group and the hospital when one's own hospital stay comes to an end.

Much of an inpatient therapist's time and thought goes into enabling the group and its members to deal with those adaptive tasks. Clarifying which adaptive task is primary at any given time involves the art of listening and of collecting data from other parts of the hospital. We discuss the art of listening more fully in Chapter 6. It is sufficient to note at this point that to understand the adaptive tasks of the group and its members, it is important that the therapist be aware of what is happening on the hospital floor as well as in the group. For instance, if a group that is normally very verbal becomes anxious and withdrawn, it can be very helpful if the therapist knows that a patient, known to the members but not a member of the group, made a suicide attempt the previous evening. By connecting that event with the mood of the members, the therapist may enable each patient to cope with that event, and in so doing, deal with the anxious and withdrawn mood of the group members at the same time.

In dealing with those adaptive tasks the individual patients bring to the group the assets and liabilities we discussed in the previous chapter. That is, the nature of the members' defensive systems, the organization of their internal objects, the level of their self-esteem will strongly affect how they perceive and respond to each other, the therapist, and their adaptive tasks. Patients, for instance, whose primary mode of defense is to deny, will cope with the various adaptive tasks within the group by denying their existence or their impact. Someone who uses projection and whose internal objects are cruel and harsh may view the therapist or other group members as cruel and harsh, even when it is clear to others that they are not. For that patient, the adaptive task of building trust will be particularly difficult. Another patient whose arrogance covers a very low self-esteem may relate to other group members by putting them down to maintain that defense. In summary, the group members will behave in ways that are reflective of who they are and of the problems that led to their hospitalization.

INTERACTIONS AMONG GROUP MEMBERS

Group therapy is unique in that many patients are present and interacting together. The interactions that take place between and among the members are central to any therapy group. They give the group its life and character. They also generate much of the material that is used in therapy. The spontaneous interactions among the members of a therapy group are analogous to the free association process in individual therapy. As the members interact with one another they frequently generate information, situations, and experiences that would not surface through direct reporting or in general conversation. Also, in these interactions the character styles of the various members get acted out and are, therefore, available for observation and examination.

For example, when a new member joins the group this represents a crisis for both the new member and the previous members. Individuals will cope with this situation in a wide variety of ways, depending on their unique histories and personalities as well as on the blend of personalities represented in the current situation. Some members may ignore the new member. Others may engage with the new member in a variety of ways, some may be challenging, whereas others may befriend and defend the new person. Each stylistic response is diagnostic.

EXAMPLE. *Dorothy had been hospitalized the day before and entered the group in a weepy and dependent manner. She drew a great deal of group attention from her obvious distress. Fran immediately introduced herself and made certain that Dorothy was introduced to all members of the group. She offered a Kleenex and was full of interest and sympathy for "poor Dorothy."*

Eric, the last addition to the group, was cold and uninterested. Foregoing his usual gregarious style, he never made eye contact with Dorothy, never spoke to her, and obviously was furious that she was now a member of the group.

Each of the other members of the group had their own responses to Dorothy's joining, but Fran and Eric are sufficient to demonstrate the point. Fran was hospitalized because she had a major depression when her only child left home for college. Fran had been the oldest child in her family of origin, and she had taken on a great many maternal responsibilities for the many siblings that followed her since her mother had been very depressed and unable to carry on her mothering functions adequately. Although this was a source of anguish and anger for Fran, it also became a foundation for her personality. Her "niche" in life was a mothering one. She poured herself into the role of mothering her own child, and she did a good job of it. But she was unable to cope with the vacuum created by the loss of the child to college. Dorothy represented a new younger sibling, or a new "baby," and Fran instantly reverted to mothering behavior and began taking care of the newest and most needy.

Eric, on the other hand, had been the youngest in his family, and he had been fawned over and given very special attention as the last of five children. Being the newest member of the group was a very familiar and beloved position for him. He had been hospitalized because of his depression when his first child was *born*. Whereas Fran had natural responses available for mothering a child, for Eric the child represented unacceptable competition for the love of his wife. Now Dorothy represents much the same threat, and he demonstrates how difficult it is for him to share.

The new member also brings his or her own historic behaviors to the joining of the group. Some may join and very quickly reveal their difficulties without being invited; some may remain aloof and uncommunicative. It is important for the therapist to remember that all these reactions are not random. Rather, they are behaviors designed to respond to the crisis facing all members of the group.

Furthermore, the situation is complicated by the recognition that the interactions among members generate their own adaptive tasks as well. In the illustration the group members are not simply saying "hello" to a new patient, they are saying hello to a patient who enters the group in a certain way. Dorothy's particular style evoked particular responses in Fran, Eric, and all the others. And those responses, in turn, triggered yet other responses.

If Dorothy entered the group angrily rather than dependently, then the members would be coping with different stimuli and would demonstrate different reactions depending on their previous experiences with anger. Passive or depressed members, for instance, may cope with the situation by using the angry patient to give expression to their own feared anger. They may do this by saying or doing things that further provoke the new patient's anger. In other words, in coping with a particular adaptive task one or more patients may attempt to solve the problem by developing particular kinds of relationships with other patients.

In summary, adaptive tasks generate interactions among members, and those interactions generate further adaptive tasks and so on, resulting in the development of particular kinds of relationships between and among members. As if the task of the therapist was not complicated enough, many times these adaptive roles are used by one or more members in the service of resisting treatment and invoke resistant behaviors in other members.

The relationships that develop among group members are the result of the nature of the adaptive tasks involved and the psychological makeup of the persons who are interacting. The defenses, internal objects, levels of self-esteem, and previous life experiences of the members not only affect how each may perceive and respond to others, but they also profoundly influence the actual relationships that develop between members. In our example, for instance, the relationship between the angry patient and the passive and depressed patients reflects the inner worlds of all the parties involved and, at the same time, helps to maintain those inner worlds. To cope with their anxiety the passive and depressed members project their anger into the new member who gives it expression. This enables the passive and depressed members to keep their anger split off from themselves and yet also identify with it in the angry patient. Conversely, the angry patient splits off the frightened or depressed side of him or herself and projects it into the passive and depressed members, thus managing to keep an unwanted part of the self split off. These complex sets of relationships, often generated, as in this instance, by splitting and projective identification, are sometimes called collusive relationships,[4] because there is an unconscious agreement by all parties involved to maintain a particular intrapsychic and interpersonal status quo. This maintains the pathology of all concerned. Frequently, those collusive relationships are isomorphic with the families of origin, or of particular relationships within those families of origin, of the participants. Thus, the members' unresolved familial conflicts from the past or present, current defenses, and internal objective organizations come together in the here-and-now relationships in the group. The interactions within the group contain and are, in part, shaped by the members' history and pathology.

The existence of such collusive relationships within a group also underscores the importance of considering the interpersonal as well as the intrapersonal or intrapsychic when leading an inpatient group. To focus simply on the anger of a particular member and overlook the relationships that intersect with that member is to miss an opportunity to help a number of members deal with significant concerns. It is also likely that a purely individual focus would be futile because of the need of so many members to maintain that member's anger and disown their own.

Not all relationships among inpatient group members are collusive. Some are empathic and understanding, and offer support and even insight. Another member of our group, for instance, may have recognized the anxiety contained within the new member's anger and responded in a quite different way. He may have told the new member that he understood how frightened she was, because he had felt the same way when he entered the group. Such an intervention is likely to reduce the new member's anxiety, and lead to mutual, overt identification and bonding between those two members, in contrast with the covert or unconscious identification and bonding of collusive relationships.

In summary, the interactions among members of an inpatient group are generated by the members' adaptive tasks and by the defensive use of those tasks. The responses to those adaptive tasks lead to networks of relationships that can provide support, shared experiences, and identifications. They also lead to networks of relationships that are collusive in nature and contain the history and pathologies of the members. Those latter relationships also provide an opportunity for understanding and change.

THE GROUP

The therapy group emerges out of the interactions of the group members and will grow and change over time, and possibly die, as do other living systems.[5-10]

THE BEGINNING OR DEPENDENCY PHASE

In the process of growing and changing groups show many patterns that are isomorphic with the growth and development of individuals. In the early phase of a group's life, for instance, the primary concern of the members is that of bonding and forming a whole cohesive unit.[11] In this early phase the focus of the members is on such things as saying "hello," finding shared qualities and experiences, comparing symptoms, learning the rules of membership, finding out who's who, and so on. In a word, the members are building a sense of trust and mutuality. During this phase differences among members are usually ignored or minimized. If unpleasant things are talked about, they are frequently described as being outside the group. The members may talk about bad things happening on the floor, or of bad treatment by the administration, in contrast with the good things happening in the group. At other times members may talk about poor treatment in previous hospitals, in contrast with the good treatment in the present hospital. In the beginning phase, the members facilitate bonding by focusing on their similarities and on that which is "good" and exclude or split off that which is different or "bad" and place it outside the group.

These events should not be viewed by the therapist as problematic. The development of a sense of mutuality and "goodness" in the group reduces anxiety, fosters trust, bonding, and safety that can enable the members to better tolerate the frustrations and difficulties that will arise later. Similarly, the idealization of the therapist, which often takes place during this phase, should not be frowned on or discouraged because it also fosters the same bonding, trust, and sense of safety.[12]

The beginning phase of the group is not confined to the opening sessions of the group. It is repeated every time a new member is added, though the process is not usually as long as when the group first begins. Because of the rapid turnover of membership, the beginning phase is repeated many times in an inpatient group.

Most people in outpatient groups find the beginning phases of a group fairly pleasant, even enjoyable, despite some initial anxiety about entering the group or meeting new members. Although this can also be true in an inpatient group, often it is not, particularly if it is a lower functioning group.[13–15]* One patient, for instance, had to observe her group from outside the door of the group room for three sessions before venturing to sit in the same room as the group. She then sat in the same room as the group for several sessions before she actually joined. Once she joined she became a very staunch member. Other members have been known to enter and leave several times before actually feeling able to stay for a full session. The adaptive task of forming or reforming a group is often more unusual and sometimes more difficult in an inpatient

---

*See also Chapter 5.

setting. The process of bonding and establishing a sense of belonging is very threatening to some patients, particularly if they have difficulty maintaining their own personal boundaries or if those boundaries have frequently been infringed on by others. In inpatient groups the initial task is often not the developing of basic trust, but rather the overcoming of basic distrust.

Bion[16] described the beginning phase of a group as the dependency phase because it operated under assumptions that emphasize the members' dependency on the leader, many of which we have just described. The primary assumption is that the therapist–leader will take charge of the group, take care of the members, and provide answers to all their problems. A corollary of this assumption is that the members are as one, so that their similarities are emphasized and their differences minimized. This is the most common phase in inpatient groups, and, as we discuss in the next chapter, it is also a central characteristic of the whole unit.

THE REACTIVE PHASE

In most instances, the anxiety that is generated by belonging to a group becomes apparent during the second phase of the group's life. In response to the fear of belonging and the corollary threat of losing one's identity, members begin to emphasize their differences and protest the rules of the group and the way in which it is being run.[17] From the perspective of the group, it is that time when its members begin to differentiate. In coping with this adaptive task the group members often reverse the split mentioned earlier. That is, they view other parts of the hospital as being good and the group as bad. They may talk of the wonderful help they are getting from their individual therapists in contrast with the ineffectiveness of their group therapist, or speak of how good the groups were in another hospital in contrast with the groups in *this* hospital, and so on.

Again, this protest should not be considered problematic. It helps some members to establish clearer interpersonal boundaries, enables others to express anger appropriately, and above all can increase the level of trust and safety in the group. This is particularly true if the therapist is seen as being able to tolerate the members' anger and frustration and to manage and limit untoward verbal and physical acts of aggression. Members learn that the group is a safe place to talk about and reveal aspects of themselves they cannot talk about or reveal elsewhere. They also learn that it will help them control aspects of themselves they may have had difficulty controlling in the past.

The splitting described in the preceding sections of this chapter appears frequently and in many varied forms in a group's life, particularly in inpatient groups. It is one of the major ways in which groups organize themselves to cope with their numerous adaptive tasks. Knowing this can greatly assist the group therapist in listening to the group and in knowing how to intervene. For instance, ambivalence in a group is frequently dealt with by splitting. Suppose a group therapist announces that she will be taking a vacation for several weeks during which time another member of the staff will be leading the group. In such a situation, it is not unusual for some members to ask for details about the new therapist, or to share information about that person, often telling others, with some excitement, how good they are. By contrast, other members may become silent and withdrawn. If they speak at all, it may be in an angry or depressed manner. Clearly, the group has split the ambivalence about the therapist's announcement. One part of the split gives voice to the relief that there will be someone to replace the leader, and that they will be taken care of, whereas the other gives voice to the shared anger and disappointment at being abandoned. On occasion, most members may give expression to the manic aspects of the ambivalence, whereas only one or two may carry the depressed and angry side. For this reason, it is important that the therapist pay attention to members who remain silent. Often they are carrying the unspoken part of a group's ambivalence. When both aspects of splits within groups are given voice and made overt the group members become better able to contain some of the ambivalence within themselves, something that is often difficult for members of inpatient groups.

THE MATURE PHASE

Integration of the split between oneness and separateness, between "good" and "bad" brings the group to its next phase.† During this

---

† This reflects one of the paradoxes of the complex relations between a group and its members. Namely, that it is possible for a group to attain a greater degree of integration than its members may be able to do individually (see the organization of the community meeting in Chapter 8). The reverse is also true. An individual may maintain a greater degree of integration than the group to which he or she belongs.

phase of the group's life members feel relatively safe. They have developed a reasonable degree of trust and feel that they can belong and at the same time be recognized and respected as separate persons. The group's boundary has become firmly but not rigidly established or reestablished. The members have also moved beyond a stage of simply sharing their experiences, or criticizing the group, to attempting to understand their experiences together.[18]

> EXAMPLE. *An inpatient group for young women suffering from anorexia met for their usual 9:00 a.m. meeting. The group began very slowly and with considerable resistance. One patient had her eyes closed, another was yawning, and yet another was curled up in a ball. After a short period, one member who had been quiet at the beginning of the session, became quite talkative and voiced some of the members' wishes to be taken care of. She talked in jest of asking her mother to bring her bed into the hospital. After this others began to complain about how hard it was to talk in the group because "the group" could not be trusted. The members then began to make suggestions as to how they might change things. One member suggested they should spend more time doing things together. Another said she wanted support from the group. Another member, Ellen, said the group wasn't safe because not everyone talked and then began to attack a silent member. She condemned her for her anger at the lunch table pointing out how it drove everyone away. The therapist inquired gently as to why that upset Ellen so much. After a moment, Ellen replied, "Because she reminds me so much of myself and how I used to provoke my mother." The accused patient was then able to talk about being unable to trust the group because she felt she was so bad.*

In this illustration, with some gentle prodding from the leader, the group had been able to move from a protest phase replete with splitting and projections, to a position where they were able to integrate the splits, work cooperatively, and examine unwanted aspects of themselves.

Not all inpatient groups pass through all these phases, though many do. Some groups, particularly those with more impaired patients, may remain at the first phase. The group therapist should not be discouraged by that fact. To enable a group of severely regressed patients to connect with each other and share similar experiences is no mean achievement for either the therapist or the group members. It is also helpful for the group members, often reducing the amount of chaotic behavior on the unit and enabling the group members to make better use of their hospital experience.[19]

TERMINATION

The last phase that has to be dealt with in inpatient groups is the termination phase. Terminations happen steadily throughout the life of an inpatient group, even while the group members are also trying to build attachments. Thus, it is not uncommon for an inpatient group to pass through several group phases during one session. Having spent time coping with the process of bonding and saying "hello" members of an inpatient group may then have to deal with the process of saying "good-bye." For the group therapist this means being aware of both those who are new to the group and those who are about to be discharged and seeing that adequate time is set aside for both the "hellos" and "good-byes" to be said.

There are periods of time in the group's life, however, when termination is a much more primary adaptive task than others. Because of the group members' overlapping hospital stays, there are periods when a large percentage of the group will remain relatively stable, particularly if the group is meeting on a daily basis. This period of stability is often followed by a number of sessions when a large percentage of the members will be terminating. Thus, inpatient groups are usually cyclical in nature. They begin, settle down to whatever developmental phase they will reach, then terminate a large percentage of their members, become somewhat disorganized, and then reform again, and so on.

Overall, inpatient groups have some of the characteristics of both open-ended therapy groups and short-term therapy groups. Their cyclical course of beginnings and endings is short-term in nature, but the fact that the groups continue indefinitely from generation to generation of patients gives them some of the characteristics of open-ended groups. These latter characteristics make it possible for an inpatient group to carry its culture forward through those generations and thus provide some stability despite the rapid turnover of patients.

RECIPROCITY OF DEVELOPMENT AND CHANGE

We have observed that who the members are affects how they interact with each other. We have also noted that the group emerges out of those interactions among the members. Thus, changes in the members and in the interactions among those members changes the character of the group. The reverse is also true. As the group changes and matures it also influences and changes the members and their interactions with one another. That is, there is a reciprocal interchange of influence between the group members and the group-as-a-whole. Among other things, this means that every adaptive task involves the group at all levels; individual, interactional, and group-as-a-whole. It also means that at whatever level therapists choose to intervene, those interventions have repercussions at all other levels of the group as well.

For instance, in Ellen's group, the therapist's intervention enabled Ellen to take responsibility for her anger at another member. It also reduced the collusive nature of the relationship that was developing between Ellen and the other patient. Following the change in that interaction the tone of the group also changed and became more cooperative and the behavior of other group members changed. Another patient was then able to turn to the group and ask them to help her deal with her mother who was always making excuses for her.

The reciprocity observed among the various systems and subsystems of the inpatient group can also be observed between the group and the larger system of which the group is a part. That larger system includes the group program, the hospital unit, and the hospital. Just as the individual members of a therapy group are affected by the organization of the group to which they belong, so the therapy group and its members are profoundly affected by the context in which the group is set. In the next chapter, we examine the psychiatric hospital or unit and its relationship to the therapy group.

REFERENCES

1. P. B. de Mare, *Perspectives In Group Psychotherapy: A Theoretical Background* (New York: Science House, 1972).

2. R. Langs, *The Technique Of Psychoanalytic Psychotherapy, Vol I* (New York: Jason Aronson, 1973), p. 281–283.

3. J. Frosch, *The Psychotic Process* (New York: International Universities Press, 1983), pp. 387–404.

4. J. Willi, *Couples in Collusion* (New York: Jason Aronson, 1982).

5. W. G. Bennis and H. A. Shepard, "A Theory of Group Development," In *From Group Dynamics To Group Psychoanalysis*, edited by M. Kissen (New York: John Wiley, 1976), pp. 145–168.

6. W. R. Bion, *Experiences In Groups* (New York: Basic Books, 1959).

7. M. Day, "The Natural History of Training Groups," In *From Group Dynamics to Group Psychoanalysis*, edited by M. Kissen (New York: John Wiley, 1976), pp. 135–144.

8. H. Kellerman, *Group Psychotherapy And Personality: Intersecting Structures* (New York: Grune & Stratton, 1979), pp. 61–90.

9. W. B. Tuckman, "The Developmental Sequence In Small Groups," *Psychol. Bull.* 63 (1965):384–399.

10. J. S. Rutan and W. N. Stone, *Psychodynamic Group Psychotherapy* (New York: Macmillan, 1985), pp. 31–52.

11. Rutan and Stone, *Psychodynamic Group Psychotherapy.*

12. J. S. Rutan and C. A. Rice, "The Charismatic Leader: Asset or Liability?" *Psychother.: Theory, Research and Practice* 18 (1981):487–492.

13. H. S. Leopold, "Selective Group Approaches With Psychotic Patients In Hospital Settings," *Am. J. Psychother.* (1976):95.

14. R. W. Betcher, C. A. Rice, and D. M. Weir, "The Regressed Inpatient Group in a Graded Group Treatment Program, *Am. J. Psychother.* 36 (1982):229–239.

15. I. D. Yalom, *Inpatient Group Psychotherapy* (New York: Basic Books, 1983), pp. 275–312.

16. W. R. Bion, *Experiences in Groups* (London: Tavistock Publications, 1961).

17. Rutan and Stone, *Psychodynamic Group Psychotherapy.*

18. Rutan and Stone, *Psychodynamic Group Psychotherapy.*

19. Betcher, Rice, and Weir, "The Regressed Inpatient Group in a Graded Group Treatment Program."

4

The Psychiatric Hospital

Hospitals can be conceptualized as large groups. Thus, the knowledge that group therapists have about the workings of smaller groups often can be applied productively to the hospital itself. In this chapter we examine some of the dynamics of the hospital as a large group.

THE HOSPITAL AS A HEALING COMMUNITY

The psychiatric hospital is made up of a variety of smaller treatment systems, or subsystems. For example, in a hospital a person may receive various types of intense therapy such as group psychotherapy, individual psychotherapy, family therapy, occupational therapy, and medication. A patient's concerns may also be explored thoroughly over time by a variety of professionals using such things as psychological tests, medication trials, EEG's, blood tests, and daily observations of behavior. All those procedures are important ingredients in the treatment and healing of the patients in the hospital, and the manner in which they are carried out contributes to the general culture and ambience of the hospital. Like other living systems, the hospital system emerges out of the interactions among its parts.

It is equally true that the parts of a living system are shaped and changed by the system of which they are a part. Thus, the efficacy of the various treatments and observations of patients is profoundly affected by the particular hospital in which they take place. Ideally, a psychiatric hospital is a healing community, but – depending on how it is run – it may be pathogenic. When it is pathogenic, the finest treatments available are likely to be ineffective or severely compromised. It is analogous to the early experiences in medical hospitals. Before the importance of hygiene was recognized, hospitals were often the breeding ground of a variety of diseases that made patients' conditions worse rather than better. Likewise, if the importance of the social environment is not considered, a psychiatric hospital may make the illnesses of patients worse rather than better. In such an environment it is very difficult to run a group effectively.

> EXAMPLE. *A large state hospital was bedeviled by competition and conflict within the staff. On one side were staff members who had been working in the hospital for many years and were primarily concerned with containing the patients, giving them medications, and keeping them quiet. Those staff members were in constant contact with the patients. On the other side were the clinical staff members, a younger and more recent staff who wanted to provide psychological treatment as well as medication and containment. The clinical staff usually saw the patients in their offices for individual appointments, or in their therapy groups. The conflict between these two groups found expression in a variety of ways. For example, the clinical staff were somewhat arrogant toward the more established staff who, in turn, gave patients off-grounds passes during times they were supposed to be in groups. Concurrently, violence increased among the patients and several group therapists were physically assaulted and injured.*

It is not necessary to have an "evil" staff to have a pathogenic environment. The irony of the preceding illustration is that members of both staff groups cared about their patients and worked hard and with the best intentions. Misunderstandings, poor leadership, unresolved conflicts, and ignorance about the importance of the milieu in which treatment takes place can all contribute to an environment that is pathogenic rather than healing.

Likewise, it takes more than just "good" staff to create a healing community. It takes an acknowledgment of the importance of the hospital environment in treatment and a willingness to organize that environment to benefit the patients and to facilitate their treatment. It means recognizing that hospitalization is itself a treatment; it is the primary treatment of which the other treatments, including group therapy, are a part.

In practice, hospitals can rarely be categorized into those that *are* and those that *are not* therapeutic. Rather, some may be more therapeutic and others more pathogenic. It is also true that any given hospital can be more therapeutic and healing at certain times and less so at other times. If we accept the importance of the hospital environment, then, we may view all hospitals as healing communities that over time may vary in the effectiveness with which they fulfill that healing task.

There are many ways in which a hospital may be run and managed to be an effective healing community. Examples of these are seen in the work of Foulkes,[1] Jones,[2] and Almond[3] among others. It is not our intention to suggest yet other ways by which a healing community may be run. Rather, our aim is to examine the impact of the healing community on patients and staff, and, in particular, those patients and staff involved in inpatient groups. We also examine those ingredients of a healing community that we view as necessary to the effective running of an inpatient group therapy program.

THE PATIENT IN THE HEALING COMMUNITY

Though each hospital is different and has its own ambience, nonetheless there are some important commonalities about hospital experiences from the patient's point of view. First, when patients enter a psychiatric hospital they lose many of the characteristics that distinguish them from others. Titles that provide them with status disappear or are minimized. Persons entering a hospital are no longer easily recognized as mothers, fathers, sons, daughters, plumbers, electricians, physicians, nurses, or police officers. They are recognized primarily as patients. That is, their commonality is emphasized.

Second, persons entering a hospital have usually experienced a severe regression that frequently makes it difficult for them to maintain clear distinctions between themselves and others.

Third, hospitals by definition are designed to take care of others. The functions of the staff include providing a safe environment for patients, protecting them from danger to themselves or others, providing food and sleeping accommodations, and a variety of therapies. This is true whether the staff places particular emphasis on patients participating in their own treatment or not. Encouraging patients to participate actively in their own treatment may counteract some of the dangers of the dependency group atmosphere* of the healing community, but it does not

---

* These dangers are discussed later in this chapter.

change the essential caretaking roles and assumptions of a psychiatric hospital.

Fourth, because of the rapid turnover of patients in an acute care hospital, the hospital is frequently in the process of forming and reforming.

Given those features of the psychiatric hospital, it is not surprising that the ambience of a healing community is that of the dependency phase of a group. The other phases of group development noted in the previous chapter can also be found, but the dependency phase tends to predominate. One of the primary goals of psychiatric hospital administration is to facilitate the healing capabilities of the dependency culture and to minimize the harmful effects of that culture.

ASSETS OF THE DEPENDENCY CULTURE

The existence of a dependency culture in a healing community provides many benefits for patients and can reinforce the effectiveness of therapy groups. Of the curative features that Yalom[4] noted in therapy groups, universality is particularly available in this group culture. Patients entering a hospital learn that they are not alone, that others have been where they are, and yet others have had some success in overcoming the difficulties they are facing. Such universality may facilitate bonding between persons whose emotional crisis may have driven them into isolation and fear of others. This, in turn, creates hope, which is a successful antidote to the futility that often accompanies hospitalization. In the dependency culture, patients also receive a great deal of peer support around the concrete issues of day-to-day living within the hospital. They receive advice, information, and support in coping with visits to the offices of various professionals in the hospital, and in coping with shift changes, medication side effects, visitors to the hospital, the ups and downs of their recovery process, off-ground privileges, and so on. Lastly, the patients themselves gain a great deal by being able to provide help for others as well as receiving it for themselves.[5]

DANGERS OF THE DEPENDENCY CULTURE

The dependency culture of the healing community also has liabilities for patients. For instance, patients may experience the sense of oneness within the hospital community as engulfing and threatening to any shreds of identity they may have left. In response, some patients become increasingly isolated and strongly resist any pressure to be with others. By contrast, other patients, seduced by the nurturing oneness and fantasied lack of conflict of the dependency culture, and by the loosening of their own boundaries, may become intensely bonded with another patient. Their anxiety is reduced, and any conflict that exists is seen as being outside their unique and special relationship. Other patients and staff are seen as the source of any discomfort, and these couples become unavailable for therapy, whether group or individual. This intense, undifferentiated bonding is often ended by an explosive separation that is particularly stressful to both parties. Sometimes these couples may oscillate between the two extremes.

Intense and undifferentiated bonding can also take place among a group of patients as well as between two patients, thus creating a dependency subgroup within the community. A wide variety of events may contribute to this, such as conflicts among patients, conflicts with and among staff, or the normal growth and development of the community. At times patients idealize and intensely bond with the hospital itself, and these patients have little incentive to "get well" and leave.

Sometimes a dependency culture is maintained by creating an enemy, either within the group or outside of it. If the enemy is within the group, then the members may seek to "save" or punish that person and reinforce their unity around that task. They may also seek to extrude that person and remove the "bad" from their ranks. If the enemy is outside the group, the members may seek to "convert" or to fight and destroy the enemy and thus reinforce their own "goodness" and unity. Examples of this process have been seen in the Jones Town massacre and in the Nazi Holocaust. When this process takes place in a hospital, albeit in a much less dramatic form, it can be very disruptive to the hospital community and to the group treatment program.

> EXAMPLE. *Early one morning a group therapist listened to his group complain about the behavior of Irene, a patient on the unit. The two succeeding groups complained about the same woman. She was a member of one of those groups, and in that group she lived up to the bad press she was getting. She was angry, unpleasant, and uncooperative.*
>
> *Later, the therapist heard the staff complain about the same woman. However, some of the evening staff noted that a very tight in-group had formed on the unit from which Irene was especially excluded. Not only was she excluded, but the in-group members talked about her and her*

"bad" behavior to other patients and to staff. The members of this group were very supportive of each other, spent many hours together, were pleasant to other patients, and helpful to staff. But the incessant criticizing of Irene continued and dominated the therapy groups, which remained stalemated. Irene continued to be angry, unpleasant, and uncooperative.

The group therapist led the community meeting of patients and staff later that week, and the issue was brought up for discussion. Irene raged at the rest of the patients, who complained vigorously about how she kept "poking her nose in where it wasn't wanted" and how she cruelly "put other patients down." They requested that the staff remove her from the hospital.

During the community meeting, the therapist realized that Irene's behavior was her way of protecting herself against the excruciating pain she felt in response to being excluded from the community. When the therapist offered that interpretation she softened and began to cry. Many members of the community then began to support her. The original in-group, however, remained intact and soon began to complain again. Other patients argued for a more reasonable approach and began to feel angry toward the in-group. Now they too were feeling excluded, and the in-group was becoming increasingly less pleasant. After many minutes of intense well-contained dialogue the meeting came to an end. The community was not all sweetness and light, but over the next few days the in-group gradually became integrated into the rest of the community. They still maintained relations with each other, but they were no longer exclusive and had less need to project their own intrapsychic and interpersonal distress onto another person. Irene settled down and the members of the therapy groups became able to talk about other matters.

In this case the in-group unconsciously scapegoated Irene to help deal with the lack of power they experienced as part of their hospitalization. It is important to add that the existence of an enemy does not always mean trouble within the group. A great deal can be accomplished by groups bonded to fight a common enemy, whether the enemy be devastating storms, life-threatening illnesses, or destructive regimes. But as our illustration makes clear, when enemies are created as a way of avoiding interpersonal and intrapsychic stress the results can be very damaging. In our example it seriously divided the community and aggravated the difficulties of one of its members.

The illustration also suggests that the dangers of the dependency culture can be reduced when there is a forum where the community's uneasiness can be voiced and appropriate boundaries can be reestablished. The dangers can also be reduced when the staff is aware of and able to handle the peculiar demands of dependency cultures.

Staff members are not immune to the effects of the dependency culture and their responses to it play a significant role in the effectiveness of the healing community and of the community meetings and therapy groups within it. We will discuss the relationship of the staff to the healing community later; in the meantime we will look at the special meanings the healing community and the staff can have for patients.

SPECIAL MEANINGS OF THE HOSPITAL AND ITS STAFF FOR PATIENTS

The hospital and its staff carry special meanings for the patients as a group and as individuals. The meanings that patients attribute to the staff and the hospital itself are frequently, though by no means exclusively, the result of transference. Some of those transferences fit the classical description of transference in which the group therapist or the institution are responded to as though they were significant persons or objects from the patients' pasts.

Many of the transferences that take place in a hospital are of a more primitive nature. Modern modifications of classical psychoanalytic theory have added to our understanding of the early stages of human development. The example of excessive couple and group bonding above represents what Self psychologists call narcissistic or selfobject transferences.[6] In such instances one member of the couple or the in-group may be experienced as an idealized object with whom to merge and feel good, or as an extension of the grandiose self who will mirror that grandiose self. The struggles that ensue with the rest of the hospital are struggles to defend against threats to that special bonding.

Object relations theorists would also view those events as examples of primitive transference, paying special attention to how various behaviors are geared to gain *some* type of object relatedness even when the overt manifestation seems designed to push everyone away. Irene, for example, was trying her best to maintain an object relatedness though her behaviors were difficult for others to tolerate. The success of her effort is demonstrated by how many people were preoccupied with her. In turn this allowed the others to use her as the repository for their projective identifications and she became the person into whom the bad objects, which have been split off, were projected. To complete the circle, Irene behaved in ways that confirmed the expectations of others and allowed them to hate those aspects of themselves that they could not totally disown.

The negative transference meanings that patients may give to a hospital or its staff also present a healing opportunity. The illustrations described above not only highlighted some of the difficulties that can arise when negative transference meanings become focused on particular persons or groups of persons, but also suggested that community or group discussion of those meanings can model the process of integrating "bad" and "good" objects.

Patients' transference meanings can be positive as well as negative. This was suggested in our earlier description of the dependency culture of the healing community. For instance, patients may view the hospital as the ideal home for which they have always hoped. It is experienced as the place where finally they are safe, understood, and nurtured. More commonly, strong positive transferences become directed toward specific members of staff, such as the group therapist, the individual therapist, or a nurse on the floor. Patients who have positive transferences are usually cooperative and available for the benefits of the healing community. They usually respond well to the help proffered by the staff, attend appointments regularly, and usually gain a great deal from their hospital experience. The development of such a positive transference has, on occasion, made it difficult for some patients to leave the hospital, particularly if the outside world has become the focus of the negative side of their transferences, or if that outside world holds some very real threats for them.

In addition to transference reactions, patients also give meanings to the hospital and its staff based on a realistic assessment of how they are being treated. Indeed, many of the transference meanings that patients give to the hospital may also be based on realistic assessments. If patients complain that the food in the cafeteria is bad, it may well be that it is bad. Likewise, if patients complain that they are being treated badly by certain staff, it may be that they are. Or it may be that there has been a realistic misunderstanding between the staff and the patients. If certain staff members are viewed with love and warm regard, it may be that they have indeed behaved lovingly and warmly toward their patients.

It is important to acknowledge the reality based meanings that patients give to their hospital experience. Indeed, the reality base of the patients' meanings should be examined and acknowledged before the transference meanings. If the staff overtly or covertly conveys the message that the meanings that patients give to the hospital or its staff are primarily transference meanings it renders the patients powerless. They cannot effect change in their environment. And it compromises their judgment and sense of potency, both of which are usually flagging anyway when they are in a hospital. Patients become much less able to determine for themselves what is real and what is not, which for some is a repetition of their experience in their families. When the reality base of patients' meanings has been acknowledged and dealt with, it is important to check if those realities may be the foci of a variety of other meanings including transference meanings. To fail to do so may mean missing a healing opportunity. It may also leave the group leader and staff feeling frustrated because despite their best efforts the "reality" problem may persist.

> EXAMPLE. *At a community meeting the patients complained that the kitchen staff had drastically reduced the number of orange popsicles in the refrigerator, adding other flavors. They felt that was rather unfair, particularly as the orange ones were so popular. The few orange ones now disappeared instantly, whipped away by those who got there first. The community meeting leader appreciated the patients' concerns as he too liked the orange popsicles. After some discussion the cook agreed to return to the original ratio of orange popsicles to other flavors. The spirit of the community meeting picked up and the members moved on to discuss a number of other concerns of a similar nature. Each problem was dealt with in turn. But they seemed endless, and many more than the leader had come to expect. Furthermore, almost all had to do with food. After giving the matter some thought, the leader noted the important concerns the members were raising, but added that they all had to do with getting less than they were used to, or with not getting enough. So he wondered aloud if they felt the same way about the staff, given that it was summer and many were away on vacation. The food concerns were dropped and the members talked at length about what it was like to have less staff around, about feeling left, neglected, and of being at risk.*

THE STAFF IN THE HEALING COMMUNITY

Staff members are also affected by the nature of the healing community in which they work. Psychiatric hospitals are very special places. It is important to assess continually just how staff members are being affected by the hospital culture.

ASSETS AND LIABILITIES OF THE HEALING COMMUNITY FOR STAFF MEMBERS

In an effective staff, members often experience the same sense of universality and oneness with their colleagues that the patients share with each other. They are reminded that they are not alone as they work on the floors, or lead groups of patients struggling with overwhelming difficulties. They learn that other staff members also feel frustrated or disillusioned or worse when, despite their best efforts, some patients or groups make little headway, others get worse and, on occasion, some patients injure or kill themselves. Similarly, they can also share with their colleagues the pleasure of seeing their groups work well, of seeing some patients overcome paralyzing depressions or the isolation of catatonia and go home. Lastly, staff members learn a great deal from each other. They share skills, techniques, and ideas as they talk about their groups or otherwise work together to help the patients.

As with patients, the dependency culture can present some dangers and difficulties for the staff. In a healing community staff and patients co-exist close to one another both physically and emotionally. The problems the patients struggle with are human problems and are usually shared, to some degree, by staff members as well. Staff members may find that working with seriously troubled patients is like working close to troubling parts of themselves. That shared human experience, together with the nature of the dependency culture, often makes the maintenance of personal and interpersonal boundaries difficult for us as well as for our patients.

Many staff members can handle that degree of intimacy well, but others find it very threatening. Some cope by placing emotional, if not physical, distance between themselves and the patients. They may become cold and disdainful toward patients, even arrogant. Such a posture, although understandable given the person's anxiety, is detrimental to patients. Often that posture leads to severe and unnecessary restriction of patients such as prescribing medications when talking is called for, or a variety of other angry and hostile ways of relating to patients.

Other staff members may overidentify with the patients. This may take a variety of forms, such as consistently siding with patients against administration, spending undue amounts of time with particular patients, or becoming overly involved with patients. In extreme cases staff members "fall in love" with patients. Even those staff members who maintain their boundaries well know that there are occasions when it is not easy to do so.

The unique forces present in hospital cultures also affect the relationships among staff members themselves. In a healing community, staff members can readily develop many warm and affectionate bonds with their peers. Such bonding is usually very helpful to all concerned, greatly facilitating the work and development of the healing community, and reflecting the best elements of the dependency culture. On occasion these associations lead to loving, intimate relationships that may last a lifetime.

Unfortunately, such relationships can also be abused. Working with seriously disturbed psychiatric patients leads staff to precocious levels of intimacy. Staff members are involved in frank discussions of sexuality, attraction, depression, despair, and life history as a matter of course. Often these discussions occur with other staff members who are essentially strangers, save only the work connections. Often staff members are called on, or choose to, act as co-therapists, and in these instances a type of "marriage" occurs. The staff present their work in public forums, and they often feel judged by how well their patients are doing on the ward. All these affective realities foster an unrealistic sense of closeness that often competes with the significant others that staff members have in their "outside" world.

As with patients, some staff members may disregard a variety of hierarchical and personal boundaries and use personal and sexual intimacy as a way to gain or maintain control and power over others or to manage their own terror of the intimacy of the healing community. Yet others, struggling with similar fears and desires, may use the charismatic situation[7] of the dependency culture to rule autocratically and distantly over others.

In summary, the dependency culture of the healing community can greatly facilitate the work of the staff, and, as with the patients, has much to offer the staff members themselves. There are also dangers for the staff that, if not contained, can greatly diminish the effectiveness of the hospital and the other treatment modalities within it, including group therapy.

Later, we discuss how the assets of the healing community may be reinforced, while its dangers are lessened. Now we examine the special meanings that staff members give to the hospital in which they work, and how those meanings affect the running of the hospital, and the maintenance of its health and the health of its subsystems.

SPECIAL MEANINGS OF THE HOSPITAL AND ITS SUBSYSTEMS FOR STAFF MEMBERS

The administration, the groups, the patients, and all the other subsystems of the hospital can have a variety of meanings for the staff that greatly influence how they carry out their tasks. Those meanings are often based on transference just as they are with patients. The staff's transference meanings, however, are usually more subject to correction by experience and knowledge of the hospital and its subsystems than the transference meanings of the patients. In addition, the staff are usually less regressed than the patients to begin with, and their role in the hospital is less likely than the patient's role to encourage further regression with the concomitant increase in transference meanings. Nevertheless, staff do develop transference meanings toward the hospital and its subsystems as do the patients.

> EXAMPLE. *A group therapist led an inpatient group in the presence of all staff members. This was done as part of staff training, and specifically, as a means of informing the staff about group therapy. The group met in the center of the room and the staff sat in a large circle outside the group. The theme that emerged spontaneously during the group session was, not surprisingly, how to deal with meeting in the presence of staff and with being observed.*
>
> *Following the group meeting the staff discussed their experience. Two primary themes emerged. First, the staff were strongly drawn toward the group and wanted to join in and participate. Second, the group was very different from what they had expected. Those who were unfamiliar with groups spoke of the fantasies they had had of group members confronting each other, even attacking each other and stirring up all kinds of unpleasant and unhelpful feelings. This led the staff to share other concerns they had had about groups that had made them less than enthusiastic about supporting the program.*

Transference meanings are also often directed toward the hospital itself, the directors, the owners, and the heads of departments. Administrators are easily viewed as parental figures who may nurture, punish, rescue, abandon, or help. Some staff may view the hospital as a "home away from home," whereas others may view it as stifling and limiting even though there may be little objective data supporting either of those views. Clearly, those transference meanings affect how cooperative or competitive a staff may be, and some may hamper the work of the staff severely.

Many of the meanings that staff members give to the hospital and its subsystems are also reality based. As with transference meanings, the reality based meanings and values staff members give to the hospital and its subsystems greatly influence the work they do. If the staff members believe that the hospital in which they work provides high quality services and that their work counts, they will work much more enthusiastically and effectively than if they believe their work is unimportant and the hospital provides low quality services.[8]

ESSENTIAL INGREDIENTS OF AN EFFECTIVE HEALING COMMUNITY

Given the complex dynamics of a psychiatric hospital, it is important to determine which factors reinforce the community's capacity to heal and reduce its capacity to do damage and to hinder the effectiveness of the therapy groups. A variety of factors can influence the effective running of a healing community. We address those that we consider to be of major significance.

SHARED VALUES

Modern psychiatric hospitals use a great deal of new technology, including medications, neurological tests, medical tests, psychological tests, more humane restraints, new therapy techniques, increased sophistication in diagnosis, and so on. Those advances have done much to improve the care and treatment of patients and cannot be disputed. In themselves, however, they cannot determine whether or not the technology will be used effectively and humanely. Nor can they provide the glue that enables staff to work enthusiastically and humanely with patients and with each other. That requires shared values.[9] The existence of shared values does not mean that everyone has to adhere rigorously to common belief systems that discourage differences of opinion. Quite the contrary, it is important that staff also have "simultaneously loose–tight properties."[10] That is, there should be a great deal of autonomy and decentralization of authority and at the same time a few firmly held central tenets. Thus autonomy is encouraged but not at the expense of the shared value of quality. In systems terms, hospitals must optimally regulate the degree of openness or closedness of their boundaries.

The values we suggest for a successful psychiatric hospital include the following:

The Patient Comes First. In a psychiatric hospital the patient should always come first. In application, this means that the hospital and all its programs should be geared primarily to meet the patients' needs and not those of the staff, the financial needs of the institution, or the training needs of the institution.

A corollary of this value is that the patient will be perceived and respected as a person and not as an illness to be diagnosed and treated.

Few working in psychiatric hospitals would dispute those values. But, as Bettelheim has pointed out, they are not easy values to put into practice.[11] They are difficult because of the countertransference responses that can be generated among staff members by the patients as we noted earlier. They can also be difficult because the patients themselves are often not easy to relate to, and sometimes do not want to be related to. In addition, the lives our patients live may seem intolerable to us, not just in terms of their pain, but also in terms of what they do and what they value or do not value. Under those circumstances it seems much easier to think of the patient as a particular diagnosis or set of unflattering diagnoses for which a set of treatments can be prescribed. The patient as a person can then be easily sidestepped.

A commitment to the belief that patients are first and foremost individuals can provide a great deal of support for individual staff members as they seek to maintain respectful relations with their patients. If this is part of the tone of staff meetings, case conferences, and community meetings it will filter down to other parts of the hospital, specifically to the therapy groups. Disrespect toward patients in those administrative and community meetings will also filter down to the groups and can be expected to make the leading of those groups more difficult. It may also influence the attitude of the group therapist.

> EXAMPLE. *A new worker joined the staff of a small, well-run private psychiatric hospital. He was given a position of major authority within the hospital. One of his duties was to run the community meeting, which he did with some enthusiasm. For reasons that were not immediately apparent, the community meetings began to run into difficulty. Patients continued to attend and participate, but they often left the meetings angry and hurt. The group therapy meetings that followed the community meeting were consumed by concerns about the community meeting. One group therapist found that during those group sessions he had to bite his tongue not to scold the patients for their "bad behavior." Staff also felt angry and hurt and began to miss meetings.*
>
> *Some staff, however, quickly understood the problem. They realized*

that despite the considerable competence of the community meeting leader, he had difficulty addressing the patients other than as patients. When the members of the community participated actively and sometimes forcefully in the meetings, that is, got closer to the leader and the staff, he would interpret their behavior in ways that subtly used their "pathology" to condemn them.

Some staff tried to talk with him about the matter, but he had little understanding of their concern. Ultimately, the matter reached the director of the hospital and after some further approaches the new staff person was encouraged to resign.

Fortunately, in this hospital the level of respect for the patients was such that the damage from the community meetings could be curtailed and finally stopped. Had it not been stopped the effectiveness of the hospital would have been seriously compromised.

Mutual Respect Among Staff. Probably, the single factor that most encourages respect toward patients in a hospital is that the staff members also feel respected by each other and by those in positions of authority. The application of that value has a peculiar twist in psychiatric hospitals where those responsible for the treatment of patients come from a number of different disciplines whose functions often overlap. The staff are usually made up of medication nurses, psychiatric nurses, psychiatric aides, psychiatric social workers, psychiatrists, family therapists, psychologists, and occupational therapists. Furthermore, levels of education and experience within and across disciplines usually vary widely.

The areas of overlap within those disciplines provide the staff with a shared language that facilitates communication and cooperation; sometimes it leads to friendly rivalry. At other times it leads to major battles over turf and power, with an emphasis on differences. Specifically, there are battles over who is in charge of patient care, who gives orders, and who carries them out. Such tension can make it difficult to maintain an attitude of respect. The illustration earlier describing how the newer clinical staff at a state hospital found their groups undermined by the more established staff reflected that lack of respect between the disciplines, as well as differences in tenure. Neither staff respected the other staff's capacity to do their job, and the patients suffered. However, where a staff has a forum and their input can be shared and accepted as valuable, a major step has been taken to create an attitude of respect between the disciplines and the work done by each of them. In such an environment, group therapists recognize that their work is respected and supported, and they in turn usually respect and support the work of their colleagues.

USE OF AUTHORITY IN BOUNDARY MAINTENANCE

Another necessary ingredient in a successful healing environment is the optimal use of boundaries. Optimally maintained boundaries free people to do their tasks – the patients can be patients and staff can be staff. The sets of shared values we have just discussed can go a long way in fulfilling that task. When we respect our patients and our colleagues we are less likely to isolate them unnecessarily or to step on their toes or otherwise use and abuse them.

One of the major regulators of boundaries in a psychiatric hospital is authority. Authority and its role in an organization is ambivalently held. Often the concerns around this issue reflect a belief that authority is inimical to freedom of choice. Sometimes it can be, and we have given a number of examples in which authority has been so abused. Authority, and the power that goes with it, however, does not have to mean power over others, rather it can mean power to effect, to bring about, to make possible. When viewed from this perspective, refusal to use authority can be as damaging to a system's boundaries as using it abusively.

> EXAMPLE. *Iris, head of a group therapy program, asked her colleagues in a supervision group for help with her program. Her basic questions were: "Why are patients not attending the groups?" and "Why are the group leaders on my staff fighting among themselves?" Her colleagues explored her situation thoroughly, and the following story emerged. She had gone to the hospital director stating that she would like to begin a group therapy program. The director listened, thought it was a good idea, and said, "go ahead and do it." She started enthusiastically and groups were formed. Soon, however, the group program faltered. There were fewer and fewer referrals for the groups. Those who had been referring patients at the beginning were referring fewer patients and many others never referred at all. Attendance at the groups was also poor. Iris and her staff then became angry at the hospital because they were not receiving referrals. The supervisory meetings often became complaining sessions about the hospital, and the group therapists felt isolated from their colleagues. Finally, the group therapists became angry with Iris. Analysis of this situation revealed that the director had effectively given Iris enough rope to hang herself. He had given her permission but had failed to back it with his authority. He had not taken steps to see that the group program was effectively incorporated within the hospital as a viable treatment mode. Iris had also failed to ask for or to clarify the nature of his support.*
>
> *The reciprocal failure of the director and the head of the group program to use the power of the office to support the program meant that it became*

> *annexed from the rest of the hospital treatment. In systems terms, an almost impermeable boundary between the group program and the rest of the hospital severely limited exchanges between the two systems. Other staff were puzzled by this "special" program, were unsure what it was about, became jealous of the "in group," and did not trust them sufficiently to refer patients. Inevitably, the group program had begun to die.*

The judicious use of authority is important in maintaining adequate boundaries within the hospital so that persons and departments may function freely and creatively, and yet give and receive adequate input to and from their environment so that they may survive and also contribute to the effective work of the whole. Patients need to be free to be patients and not have to be burdened with satisfying the personal needs of the staff. But they must also have access to staff to benefit from being in the hospital. To be effective a therapy group needs to have a time and space within which it can operate without interruption. It must also be an integral part of the hospital so that it can receive new patients and have backup support for crises. The group therapist must be free to lead the group without intrusions from other parts of the hospital but must also have access to information about the ongoing treatment of the members and a way to share information about the members' group experience with colleagues. Likewise the therapy groups themselves must have clear boundaries. For example, there should be no doubt about who is in the group and who is not. There must be strong boundaries that protect against staff or nonmember patients intruding into the group during meetings, and yet there must be enough permeability so that new members can join and information can flow in to the group leaders. The group boundaries must include clear beginnings and endings, and a clear set of expectations of safe behavior. This framework helps the members feel free to express what is on their minds.

Authority can be used to enable the community to integrate the "loose–tight properties" observed in the successful organizations.[12] Clear and firm boundaries facilitate autonomy. The setting in which group therapy takes place has a profound effect on how effective that treatment will be. In this chapter we have indicated some of the complexity of the hospital setting and the various forces that impinge on patients and staff. We have also discussed some ways by which the assets of the hospital may be reinforced and the risks minimized. In the next chapter, with this material as a backdrop, we discuss the process of establishing a group therapy program in a psychiatric hospital.

REFERENCES

1. S. H. Foulkes, *Therapeutic Group Analysis* (New York: International Universities Press, 1964), pp. 187–219.

2. M. Jones, *The Therapeutic Community* (New York: Basic Books, 1968).

3. R. Almond, *The Healing Community: The Dynamics of the Therapeutic Milieu* (New York: Jason Aronson, 1974).

4. I. D. Yalom, *The Theory and Practice of Group Psychotherapy*, 3rd edt (New York: Basic Books, 1985).

5. I. D. Yalom, *Inpatient Group Psychotherapy* (New York: Basic Books, 1983), pp. 41–42.

6. H. Kohut, "The Psychoanalytic Treatment of the Narcissistic Personality Disorders," *Psychoanal. Study Child* 23 (1968):86–113.

7. J. S. Rutan and Cecil A. Rice, "The Charismatic Leader: Asset or Liability." *Psychother: Theory Research and Practice* 18 (1981):487–492.

8. B. J. Peters and R. H. Waterman, Jr. *In Search of Excellence* (New York: Harper & Row, 1982).

9. T. Watson, Jr., *A Business and its Beliefs: The Ideas That Helped Build IBM* (New York: McGraw-Hill, 1963), p. 5.

10. *Ibid.*

11. B. Bettelheim, "The Love That is Enough: Countertransference and the Ego Processes of Staff Members in a Therapeutic Milieu," in *Tactics and Techniques in Psychoanalytic Therapy*, vol II, edited by P. L. Giovacchini (New York: Jason Aronson, 1975), pp. 251–278.

12. Peters and Waterman Jr., *op. cit.*, pp. 318–325.

5

Establishing a Group Therapy Program

The thesis that in inpatient care hospitalization itself is the primary mode of treatment implies that the orientation and the organization of inpatient group therapy must be congruent with the orientation and the organization of the hospital. Therefore, before building a group program in an inpatient setting, one must take into consideration the goals, values, and organization of the hospital and how those factors interact with a group program. Specific questions to be answered are, Will the administration back a group program financially, administratively, and/or philosophically? How will the group program affect other modes of treatment? Who will be in the groups? What kind of groups make sense in this setting? Who will lead the groups? In a sentence, can there be a reasonable fit between the group program, other modes of treatment, and the hospital?

The answers depend in part on the values of the particular hospital in which the group program is to be built and, in part, on how the group therapist sets about negotiating the building of that program. One may decide, for example, that the values and the orientation of the hospital are so different from those of group therapy that establishing a group program would be out of the question. However, it is much more likely that the question will be how does the therapist negotiate for and establish a group program in a specific hospital? Or how does the therapist renegotiate and reorganize the group program so that it may be more vital and effective?

The first steps are taken with the hospital administration.

RELATIONSHIP OF THE GROUP PROGRAM
TO THE HOSPITAL ADMINISTRATION

Hospital administration refers to those persons directly responsible for the administration of direct services and the overview of the staff who provide those services.

ALLIANCE BUILDING

The initial task, particularly if there has never been a group program in the hospital before, is to build alliances with the administration and then with the staff. The primary means of doing this is through educating and informing. This often takes the form of talks with the administration, during which the therapists supply information about how groups work, what they can offer to the hospital, and what they can offer to the patients. This process should include listening to the needs and concerns of the administration and inviting input from them about the proposed group program. There may also be more formal components, such as visits to other hospitals that have group programs, or discussions with consultants or visitors from other successful inpatient group programs.

Once the process of informing the administration is well underway it is important to inform the rest of the staff. This can be done informally over lunch, in staff meetings, and during case conferences. More formal ways of informing the staff, many of whom may not be familiar with group therapy, include presentations at staff meetings by people knowledgeable in the field, demonstration groups, attendance at group therapy conferences, and so on.

The essential ingredients are that the administration and the staff be kept constantly informed during the process of building the group program, that they be given an opportunity to provide input, and that that input be respected and incorporated where possible. The end result is an alliance between the group program, the administration, and the rest of the staff, thereby significantly increasing the likelihood of the program's success.

CONTRACTS

Any group, be it a government, a business, a hospital, or a therapy group must have a clear and consensually agreed upon contract to work effectively.[1] The goals, the "rules of the game," and the parameters of groups must be clearly defined for maximum efficiency. Sometimes contracts exist to define various boundaries for the groups involved. Inpatient therapy groups need *two* contracts—the inside contract and the outside contract. Each contract deals with one of the two faces of the group boundary. The inside contract is the agreement between the group leader and the members about how the group shall be run. This is dealt with more fully in the next chapter. The outside contract defines the relationship between the group and the rest of the hospital. To be effective these contracts must be congruent.

The Outside Contract. The outside contract is negotiated between the group therapist, or the group therapy program director, and the administration. It establishes criteria that will help maintain and reinforce the group's boundaries, principally by means of four central ingredients.

1. Group therapy must be congruent with the overall treatment program of the hospital or the unit. When this happens the goals, tasks, and interventions of the group therapist are supported by the other clinicians, and patient attendance at the groups is encouraged. If it is not congruent therapy groups will not work effectively and may not even survive. Lack of congruence inevitably leads to conflict between other staff and group therapists. One common symptom of this problem is absenteeism in groups as patients play out and exploit the differences among the staff. When this fundamental congruence is missing, groups also suffer from inadequate referrals, which results in small and ineffective groups.
2. Group therapy shall be a primary treatment mode, and not subservient to other treatments. One important result of this aspect of the contract is the reduced likelihood of patients having their group time preempted by other treatments. This, in turn, reinforces the boundaries of the groups.
3. As a consequence of (2), group boundaries must be respected by all staff and patients. Group sessions shall not be entered by anyone other than members and leaders, patients will not be

called out of their groups for visitors, other treatment modes, appointments, or other duties. When group therapy is undervalued, groups are all too often interrupted by visiting physicians, medication checks, unexpected guests, and staff whims. Usually these interruptions occur without malevolent intent. Groups are convenient places to look for patients, and when groups are viewed, consciously or unconsciously, as "less important" than other forms of treatment, it is only natural that group time be used to accomplish other things that are hard to schedule. Members of such groups do not miss the subtle message, and they in turn begin to devalue the group. Unfortunately it happens rather often in many hospitals. To develop trust and working alliances in therapy groups it is crucial that the group boundaries be respected by everyone.

4. All patients are expected to participate in therapy groups. This serves the function of validating the importance of therapy groups as a place for individuals to examine themselves and to grow. Though exceptions can be made in rare cases where it is clear that a patient may not be able to make use of a group, such as instances of severe brain damage or impulsive, violent acting out, it is important that the norm be that patients participate in groups.

This aspect of the outside contract also facilitates the assignment of patients to a group early in their hospitalization and helps to maintain groups at an optimal size. When group therapy is an optional treatment, each individual must be evaluated for group therapy in addition to their individual therapy, medications, and various other treatment modalities. It is far wiser and more efficient to begin with the assumption that all patients will be in groups and to then make exceptions for specific cases.

Implementing the Outside Contract.   Like most contracts, agreement does not make it happen, particularly as certain aspects of the contract are matters of attitude and not just practice. Clarity and overt agreement, however, are a start. Once it is put into practice and infringements are firmly and courteously dealt with, the contract gradually becomes internalized by the staff and the patients. It becomes an integral part of the community.

RELATIONSHIP OF THE GROUP PROGRAM
TO OTHER TREATMENTS

Although it is important that the boundaries of the groups be strengthened by the outside contract and not be infringed on unnecessarily by other parts of the hospital, it is equally important that group therapists respect the boundaries of other departments and treatment modalities. This general atmosphere of cooperation and coordination is worth spelling out more specifically at this point.

CONSTRUCTIVE COMMUNICATION BETWEEN GROUP THERAPISTS AND OTHERS

One simple and effective means of laying the ground rules for constructive communication relates to scheduling of group meetings. Hospitals are busy places, and it is often difficult to find a time when groups of patients can meet without conflicting with some other activity. It is important that group therapists take into consideration the time schedules of other programs. It is worth the time and effort to avoid all possible conflicts.

Once the program is underway group therapists (and directors of group therapy programs) must maintain regular dialogue with other staff members. Most important, group therapists must be in ongoing dialogue with the staff about the patients in their groups. Groups represent powerful therapeutic modalities, and group therapists are privy to important information about how patients are doing and what issues are paramount with patients at given times. This information must be communicated with other professionals in the hospital so that the patient's needs can best be served. We maintain that confidentiality is respected as long as information is kept within the hospital community, and that it is harmful to the patient to keep significant events that occur in the group secret from other relevant hospital personnel. By keeping other caretakers involved, group therapists can often gain supporters who help patients regularly attend their groups.

In addition, other staff members are valuable resources for information about the ward behavior of the group patients, information otherwise unavailable. It is vitally important for the maximum effectiveness of an inpatient group that the therapist know of particularly powerful stimuli that occur on the ward and affect the patients. Group therapists can also assist other caretakers. For example, a medication physician might ask that the group therapist assess the object relatedness or the mental status of a particular patient in a group to help him or her assess the effects of a new medication.

Group therapists can take additional steps to help reinforce the alliance between the groups and the rest of the hospital. For instance, it is often helpful to have members of the floor staff act as observers, leaders-in-training, or co-leaders of groups. Contact in this manner demystifies the groups for the staff, includes them, and increases both their willingness and their ability to support the work of the group therapists. It may also begin a process of training group therapists for the future. It is even possible to have an entire staff observe a therapy group on an occasional basis, such as having a senior therapist lead a group of patients during a case conference. In some hospitals such observations are regularly scheduled, and the increased understanding among the staff of the group process enriches their observation of patient ward behavior. Group therapy is also seen as integral to the hospital treatment program.

We have suggested specific ways in which constructive dialogue between group therapists and the rest of the hospital staff may occur. A variety of approaches are possible. Whatever the approach, it is essential that regular conversation exist between the group therapists and the rest of the staff.

COMMUNITY MEETINGS

It is also helpful to have the group therapists attend community meetings. Typically, the group therapist can offer insight into the issues that underlie these often confusing meetings. It is not uncommon for material raised in group therapy to be vented in community meetings, and by the same token for material from community meetings regularly to find its way into groups. If the group therapist can be present at the community meeting he or she is obviously much better informed about what is happening on the ward. It guarantees that a consistent message about the groups will be delivered to all patients and staff members and demonstrates that groups are part of the fabric of the hospital and a central part of the hospital treatment plan.

EFFECTIVE COMMUNICATION

The marriage of regular dialogue about the hospital's therapy groups to a clear, institutionally agreed on "outside" contract allows for an optimal flow of information in and out of the groups, while allowing their boundaries to remain firm and intact. It also creates a pro-group culture within the hospital. In such a culture

> . . . patients attend groups, talk about their groups, the staff talk about the groups, and both patients and staff know that patients are expected to attend those groups. Patients may complain about their groups, but they quickly learn that those complaints are to be taken back to their groups where they will be heard and responded to. They learn that practice not just from the staff but also from their peers.[2]

It has been our observation that where such a pro-group culture exists there is rarely any major difficulty in getting patients to attend groups.

PATIENT SELECTION

Thoughts about who should be seen in group psychotherapy vary considerably. Some suggest that group therapy is the treatment of choice for patients remarkably similar to those found in hospitals. Some behavioral/phenomenological therapists recommend group therapy for people who lead empty, dreary, and isolated lives and for others who are overdependent and overdemanding.[3,4] Others[5] have suggested that group therapy helps patients whose behavior is ego-syntonic and who, therefore, do not view themselves as responsible for the conflicts and discomforts they experience. In the group their peers let them know repeatedly how their behavior affects them, until it gradually becomes ego-dystonic and subject to change.

In contrast, others[6] use as inclusionary criteria personality characteristics that are missing, severely restricted, or temporarily annulled in inpatients. They include such characteristics as the ability to maintain a sense of self in face of the strong dedifferentiation pull of a therapy group, and to be empathic toward others.

Likewise, the criteria used to exclude people from outpatient therapy groups describe well the characteristics of patients seen in hospitals. The exclusionary criteria used by Rutan and Stone,[7] for example, are representative, and include the patient who is in an acute crisis, such as a developmental crisis (marriage, divorce), a situational crisis (death of a loved one), or a crisis of pathology (eruption of psychotic process, extreme anxiety).

Other exclusionary criteria are insufficient impulse control and sociopathy. These criteria refer primarily to people who cannot ". . . establish the minimal object relatedness that is required for a therapy group to work effectively."[8]

All of the above are commonly found among members of inpatient groups.

Taken as a whole the inclusionary and exclusionary criteria appear very confusing and less than helpful. They seem much less confusing, however, when we realize that the therapists developing the criteria often had specific groups and patients in mind. For instance, being able to maintain a sense of self in face of the regressive pull of a therapy group is essential if the patient is entering a psychodynamic, outpatient group comprised of relatively well functioning neurotic patients where regression is a necessary and desirable part of the treatment. A patient who has difficulty maintaining a sense of self, however, may do quite well in another group, with patients similar to him or herself, where the degree of regression is more contained.

Thus the most reasonable conclusion that can be drawn from clinical experience is that "At this juncture in history, . . . almost all patients are potential candidates for group psychotherapy."[9] ". . . the dispositional question is less 'Should group be considered for this patient?' and more 'For which group should this patient be considered?' and secondly 'Are there mitigating factors *against* considering this patient' for this group at this particular time?"[10]

That statement is also consistent with our thesis that all psychopathology, whatever its genesis, affects and is affected by interpersonal relations. This means much more than the simple observation that people with severe emotional problems have difficulty in getting along with others. It is an acknowledgment that whether the etiology of the patient's pathology is biological, intrapsychic, interpersonal, or all of the above, the end result is an inadequate ego organization that profoundly affects the capacity to relate to others. The therapy group provides a unique setting in which the nature of the members' limited object relations development can be observed and addressed.

Despite our conviction that almost all individuals can benefit from group therapy, however, and our conviction that even those patients typically excluded from long-term, outpatient groups might do well in the controlled environment of a hospital setting, nonetheless there are patients who do not do well in inpatient groups, or who are harmful to those groups. We agree substantially with the list set forth by Rutchick, which we have modified slightly (our changes are in italics):

1. Patients who are unable to tolerate *even* moderate external stimulation.
2. Patients whose impulse control is insufficient to offer *themselves or* other group members reasonable safety.
3. Patients who are cognitively impaired to the extent that they suffer short-term memory loss and disorientation (e.g., patients who are heavily medicated, delirious, or undergoing electroconvulsive therapy).
4. Patients who are chronically mute.
5. Patients with whom the therapist feels **excessive** discomfort.[11]

The last two exclusionary criteria need additional comment. We disagree with the practice of excluding the mute patient because the role of muteness can be understood with regard to its intrapsychic and interpersonal functions just as other interpersonal styles. Finally, as Rutchick notes, therapists cannot be helpful to patients with whom they feel excessive discomfort. In an inpatient therapy group that observation has special ramifications. The excessive discomfort that a therapist may have toward one patient will affect all other patients and severely limit the effectiveness of the group. Furthermore, members of inpatient groups do not readily distinguish their needs and experiences from those of others close to them. Thus the excessive discomfort that a leader may have toward one patient may be experienced by other members as directed at them and will greatly reduce the sense of safety in the group. It is also an unnecessary act of disrespect to one's self as a therapist to try to work with a patient who causes excessive distress. Lastly, when a particular patient causes excessive discomfort for one therapist, it does not follow that the patient should be excluded from all therapy groups. The same patient may do well in a group with another therapist, who does not experience excessive discomfort with that person.

GROUP COMPOSITION

Hospitalized patients represent a wide range of diagnoses and pathologies, ranging from fundamentally healthy individuals who have endured significant traumas that temporarily overwhelm their defenses, to chronically psychotic patients who are inadequate to live an unprotected life. Under those conditions it is difficult to get a reasonably good fit between the group and the specific members.

One helpful way to address this problem is to have a hierarchy of groups within the group therapy program.[12–14]

HIERARCHY OF GROUPS

DEFINING THE HIERARCHY

In establishing a hierarchy of groups the first task is to decide how that hierarchy shall be defined. We have developed our hierarchy of groups primarily to fit different levels of patient functioning. This is a useful criteria for a short-term setting because a judgment of level of functioning can be made quickly and accurately. Matching patients on the basis of diagnoses, as some practitioners suggest,[15] can take considerable time, often more time than is available on a short-term unit. It is worthy of note, however, that there is often a positive correlation between level of functioning and diagnostic categories, so that groups arranged on the bases of functioning are likely to be remarkably similar in the end to those arranged on the basis of diagnoses.

DETERMINING THE LEVEL OF PATIENT FUNCTIONING

When determining the level of patient functioning, it is important to take into consideration all available information about that patient. This is another occasion when input from other staff personnel is crucial. All members of the hospital staff, including secretaries, medication doctors, and mental health workers have ongoing personal contact with the patients on the ward. Each has ample opportunity to observe the functioning level of patients in everyday routine, and their consultation is valuable in determining the level at which a patient is functioning.

In addition, of course, the group therapist must also meet with the patient and draw his or her own conclusion about the level of functioning of the patient.

Level I Groups. Level I groups are designed to meet the needs of the poorest functioning and most severely regressed patients. In an acute care short-term hospital this usually means the most recently admitted patients, who often are confined to a locked unit because they are unable to moderate their own behavior. Specifically, these groups are designed for patients with severe psychotic symptoms, such as floridly paranoid ideation, hypomania, inappropriate social behavior, and severe social withdrawal; and for other patients who are unable to tolerate the anxiety engendered by larger, less structured groups. Often they are patients who have difficulty remaining seated for long periods of time.

Level I groups are smaller and more highly structured than other groups in the hospital. Like Leopold[16] and others[17–19] we have found that groups of four to six work best with patients who are this acutely troubled. Groups of three to four are often very effective. Therapists are also more active in their leadership and in the structuring of the level I group than at other levels. We discuss the specifics of the therapists' interventions in Chapter 9, "Leading an Inpatient Group," but it is sufficient to note at this point that the increased activity of the therapists and the greater structure in level I groups are designed to contain the anxiety of the patients and to create a safe environment in which the group members can relate to each other.

The goals of level I groups are important but modest. A great deal of unnecessary frustration can be created for therapists if their goals and expectations are unrealistic. We have found that the following goals can be approached, if not reached, in a level I group: (1) to strengthen the severely deteriorated ego functions of the members, (2) to enable them to relate to others in a minimal way without being totally overwhelmed or isolated, and (3) to experience respect and welcome at their basest level of functioning. In other words, the broad goal is to enable the members to begin reestablishing clear interpersonal boundaries and connections. This broad goal is often broken down into specific goals depending on the needs of the group members. Betcher, Rice, and Weir note that these specific goals usually include:

> . . . some or all of the following: to orient patients to the hospital, providing information about hospital rules, privileges, etc; to gently confront and set limits on (but not explore) distortions; to discourage inappropriate behavior, such as undressing and physical or verbal intrusiveness between members, and to encourage and reward more appropriate alternatives; to increase tolerance of small amounts of anxiety; and to help patients establish trusting relationships—first, by experiencing the leaders as non-punitive, concerned, and responsive, and then by learning to trust other patients.[20]

From the perspective of the hospital and the group program several other goals can be approached at level I. First, the safe interpersonal relations that become established within the group contribute to the establishment of cooperation, safety, and acceptance in the locked unit. Second, the level I group experience trains the members in the use of group therapy and facilitates their use of other groups later in their treatment. Third, to "graduate" most members from a level I group into a level II group with its higher expectations and goals. A brief survey of treatment effectiveness in a level I group by Betcher, Rice, and Weir[21] found that 90 percent of the members of a level I group in an acute care short-term hospital were able to move to a level II group.

Given the rapid turnover of patients in short-term acute care hospitals, and the prospect that most members of a level I group will graduate to a level II group, it is important that these groups meet at least five times a week. Persons entering a hospital in acute psychological distress are constantly being bombarded by new and stressful experiences and need as much consistent support as possible. Furthermore, since the memory traces of more primitive patients are tenuous at best, regular meetings are needed to keep the group and its relationships within their awareness.

In large hospitals it is helpful to have two categories of level I groups, one being for those patients who are experiencing acute emotional distress such as we have described above, and one for those who have a history of severe and chronic emotional illness. This modified model allows chronic patients to remain in the same group throughout their hospital stay, where they can benefit from the stability and reduced demands of the "chronic" level I group. The cogency of this modification is confirmed by the study noted earlier in which Betcher, Rice, and Weir[22] found that fewer than 10 percent of patients in an acute care hospital did not graduate from a level I group to a level II group before being discharged from the hospital. Examination of those patients' records revealed that they were almost always patients who had chronic emotional difficulties, usually chronic schizophrenia.

Level II Groups. Level II groups are for patients who have begun to recompensate, are not actively psychotic, and are not currently dangerous to themselves or others. They are usually no longer, or may never have been, in the locked unit. In the main, they are able to tolerate the stress, and the greater responsibilities and advantages of the open unit. They are able to sit in a group for periods of forty-five to ninety minutes and can bear the anxiety generated by the relative lack of structure of a level II group when contrasted with a level I group.

Many members of level II groups will have graduated from a level

I group, where they will have learned some of the basic skills of group membership. A few begin their group treatment at this level because when they were admitted they did not require the protection of a locked unit or the structure of a level I group.

The goals of level II groups continue those of level I groups. The broad goals of strengthening deteriorated ego functions and enabling members to reestablish clear interpersonal boundaries and connections continue. From the perspective of the hospital the level II groups, like the level I groups, facilitate cooperation and safety on the floor and ✔ reinforce other learning within the hospital. The primary difference is that these goals usually take place at a more mature level than in level I groups.

Level II groups also begin the process of education in psychotherapy in general, and in group psychotherapy in particular, that can be carried on after the patients leave the hospital. The aspects of group therapy that inpatients have found most helpful are installation of hope, group cohesiveness, altruism, and universality.[23-26] Thus, as Maxmen notes, the goals for group therapy become teaching

> . . . patients how to: (a) accept help from others, (b) recognize that one's problems are not unique, (c) realize they can help others, (d) identify one's own maladaptive behaviors, and (e) detect and avert potentially difficult situations that could aggravate symptoms. . . . to think clinically . . .[27]

In addition to Maxmen's goals, it is also possible to enable members of level II groups to understand the relationships between current behaviors and current events. The leader can enable patients to understand that their anger, sadness, or lateness to a group session may be an attempt to cope with some events taking place in the group or on the floor, like the therapist's vacation or a patient's suicide attempt.

This learning and insight not only helps the patient while in the hospital but also lays the foundation for effective treatment after discharge.

Level III and Transition Groups. Hospitalization should educate ✔ the patient to use treatment effectively after discharge, whether that treatment be medication, living in a half-way house, individual therapy, group therapy, or any combination of the above. Most patients, however, who are discharged from acute care hospitals do not continue in group therapy. Some are not appropriate candidates for group therapy and would be excluded by most current exclusionary criteria.[28] Others simply choose not to continue in therapy of any kind. Those reasons do not explain, however, why many others do not enter outpatient group therapy, particularly those who have benefited from group therapy in the hospital and would not be excluded from outpatient groups by most criteria. One explanation seems to be an unwillingness in many hospitals to seriously prepare patients for group therapy after discharge.

Level III groups address this problem. They are outpatient groups that patients join toward the end of their hospitalization and may remain in for as long as needed after discharge. If the groups are part of the hospital's outpatient unit, a referral process leading to continuity of care from hospital admission to outpatient group treatment becomes feasible. It can also greatly facilitate the sometimes problematic transition from the hospital to the "outside world," particularly if the groups contain other ex-inpatients. An example of level III groups is seen in the work of Battegay* who leads a group of ex-inpatients that has been in existence for seventeen years. The average stay of patients is eight years. A similar process has been carried out at the Appleton Unit of McLean Hospital in Belmont, Massachusetts, for alcoholic inpatients.

The functions of a level III group can be provided for patients who were members of a therapy group before entering the hospital by referring them back to their original group, unless there are some very convincing contraindications. Ideally, outpatient group treatment would continue during the hospital stay, with the patient travelling from the hospital to the group sessions as soon as it was reasonable to do so.

In hospitals where it is not possible to develop an outpatient group program, transition groups can be developed. This often happens in hospitals whose location does not make them readily accessible for long-term follow-up work. Transition groups are usually open ended in structure but time limited in membership. Members enter these groups for a limited period of time, say eight sessions, two of which may overlap with their hospital stay. This provides the members with support from others dealing with similar problems, such as anxiety about leaving the hospital, returning to their jobs, reentering their families, or separating from their families, staying on their medications, beginning outpatient therapy, looking for places to live, finding another group, and so on.

Level III groups then are concerned with the transition from the hospital to the community and with the continuity of treatment after discharge. We consider the most effective level III groups to be those

---

* See Chapter 1, p. 18.

that can provide continuity of care from hospitalization to a reasonable resolution of patients' problems. Where this is not possible, the use of a transition group is a viable, though limited, compromise.

ASSIGNMENT OF PATIENTS TO GROUPS

Patient assignment is an important aspect of any inpatient group therapy program, doing much to determine the overall effectiveness of the program. Patients should be assigned to groups by the group therapist or by someone specifically chosen for the task, particularly where a large number of groups and group therapists are involved. The person chosen for this task should have a thorough knowledge of the group therapy program, be experienced in leading groups in the hospital, have a working knowledge of events on the unit or hospital floor, and be in regular contact with the hospital staff.

Before making an assignment the therapist should consult with the ward staff for an evaluation of the patient's current condition and behavior. This can help in the choice of group level for the patient. In addition, the therapist should know the needs of the therapy groups. Some groups may have no openings, whereas another may have several. One group may need more male patients to provide reasonable gender heterogeneity, whereas another could benefit from having an emotionally expressive patient or a sad patient to better balance the affects represented in the group.[29] Knowledge of these needs of the therapy groups can enable the therapist to make a better match between the patient and the group.

After talking with the staff the therapist should meet with the patient. This meeting should be used as a means of getting to know the patient, welcoming him or her to the hospital, and informing him or her about the group therapy program in simple straightforward language. This information should specify that group therapy is part of the hospital treatment program, that all patients attend groups, that there is a group therapy contract, and the purpose of the group. The stated purpose may be simple, such as, "The purpose of the group is to help you get well and leave the hospital." For some patients it is helpful to be more specific, often by including goals that have been set for the patients' behavior on the unit, or requests made by the patients themselves. They may include such things as being able to talk to other people, being able to control one's temper, or being able to sit still, and so on. Usually, the goals become refined as the nature of the patient's interpersonal difficulties become clearer in group. Specific details about group assignment should be given at this meeting, including data about time, place, leadership, and relevant information about the current life of the group to which the patient is being assigned.

Because of the vast array of material a new patient faces when entering a hospital, it is helpful to write down the name of the group and the place, days, and times when it meets. Patients often carry this information around with them to help orient them to the hospital and to the passage of time and days as well as to remind them of their group meetings.

Any factual questions patients may have about groups during this initial meeting should be answered clearly and directly.

It is important to be clear and direct in this initial meeting. With rare exceptions, it is unwise to invite patients to attend groups or to suggest that it is an option. Patients' anxiety and associated confusion are often very high early in their hospitalization so that communications that demand decision making, or that are vague and uncertian, tend to increase anxiety and confusion and discourage attendance at groups. Most patients respond better to a clear, friendly, and respectfully stated requirement.

Therapists must use clinical judgment in determining the best way to state this requirement. For instance, some patients will balk at the idea of entering a group. For many such patients, particularly if their concerns have been judged by staff to be primarily characterological in nature, it is best to recognize their wish not to attend, but to state the expectations clearly and firmly nevertheless. Such patients usually respond well to clearly set limits (including constantly testing them) and tend to get increasingly anxious and sometimes belligerent when the limits are not clear.

By contrast other patients may balk at the idea of entering a group because they are terrified at the thought of being that close to other people. Those patients are often schizophrenic and are concerned that they may not survive when they are with others. They fear others may consume them emotionally, if not physically. With such patients it is often helpful to devise means by which they can enter the group gradually. For example, these patients may be helped to join a group if they can observe the group from a distance, say from the doorway of the group room, before joining.

It has been our experience, however, that when the assignment is made in a direct, friendly, and respectful manner in a unit with a pro-group culture, most patients will accept their assignments fairly cooperatively, sometimes accompanied by protests but often with little protest. Usually, the protests have more to do with attempting to maintain a sense of self-respect and autonomy in a situation where patients feel they have little of either left rather than a protest against group therapy *per se*.

After the assignments have been made, the therapist must inform the staff, including the patients' individual therapists. On a small unit this may be done orally, but in larger hospitals it is very helpful to have the group assignments posted and limit oral communications to a number of key persons, such as the head nurse on the unit, the unit director, or the individual therapists. If the group therapist has any difficulties in making the assignments, it is important to let those staff members most directly involved with that patient know. Other staff can often help in overcoming the difficulties and in providing support for the group therapist should the difficulty continue.

Once the group program is launched and patients have been assigned to the groups, the primary task facing the therapist is that of leading the groups themselves, to which we now turn.

REFERENCES

1. J. S. Rutan and W. N. Stone, *Psychodynamic Group Psychotherapy* (New York: Macmillan, 1984), pp. 107–115.

2. C. A. Rice and J. S. Rutan, "Boundary Maintenance in Inpatient Therapy Groups," *Int. J. Group Psychother.* 31(1981):307–308.

3. M. Neumann and B. Geoni, "Types of Patients Especially Suitable for Analytically Oriented Group Psychotherapy: Some Clinical Examples," *Isr. J. Psychiatr. Relat. Sci.* 12(1974):203–215.

4. H. Grunebaum and W. Kates, "Whom to Refer for Group Psychotherapy," *Am. J. Psychiatr.* 132(1977):130–133.

5. J. A. Guttmacher and L. Birk, "Group Therapy: What Specific Therapeutic Advantages," *Compr. Psychiatry* 12(1971):546–556.

6. D. Zimmerman, "Indications and Counterindications for Analytic Group Psychotherapy—A Study of Group Factors," in *Group Therapy 1976: An Overview*, edited by M. L. Aronson, A. R. Wolverg, and L. R. Wolberg (New York: Stratton Intercontinental Medical Book, 1976).

7. Rutan and Stone, *Psychodynamic Group Psychotherapy*.

8. *Ibid.*, p. 87.

9. Rutan and Stone, *Psychodynamic Group Psychotherapy*.

10. *Ibid.*, p. 77.

11. I. E. Rutchick, "Group Psychotherapy." in *Inpatient Psychiatry: Diagnosis and Treatment,* edited by L. I. Sederer (Baltimore: Williams and Wilkins, 1983), p. 256.

12. H. S. Leopold, "Selective Group Approaches with Psychotic Patients in Hospital Settings," *Am. J. Psychother.* 30(1977):95–105.

13. R. W. Betcher, C. A. Rice, and D. M. Weir, "The Regressed Inpatient Group in a Graded Group Treatment Program." *Am. J. Psychother.* 36(1982):229–239.

14. I. D. Yalom, *Inpatient Group Psychotherapy* (New York: Basic Books, 1983), pp. 209–312.

15. Rutchick, "Group Psychotherapy."

16. Leopold, "Selective Group Approaches with Psychotic Patients in Hospital Settings."

17. R. Battegay, "Psychotherapy of Schizophrenics in Small Groups," *Int. J. Group Psychother.* 15(1965):316–328.

18. L. N. Cory, "Group Techniques for Effecting Change in the More Disturbed Patient." *Group* 2(1978):149–160.

19. S. R. Slavson, "Group Psychotherapy and the Nature of Schizophrenia." *Int. J. Group Psychother.* 11(1961):3–32.

20. R. W. Betcher, C. A. Rice, and D. M. Weir, "The Regressed Inpatient Group in a Graded Group Treatment Program." *Am. J. Psychother.* 36(982):229–239.

21. Betcher, Rice, and Weir, "The Regressed Inpatient Group in a Graded Group Treatment Program."

22. *Ibid.*

23. J. S. Maxmen, "Group Therapy as Viewed by Hospitalized Patients." *Arch. Gen. Psychiatr.* 28(1973):404–408.

24. R. J. Becker and M. Q. Kolit, "Curative Aspects in Hospital Group Psychotherapy." unpublished manuscript (1980).

25. C. D. Emrick and J. Silver, "Curative Factors in Hospital Group Psychotherapy." Paper presented at the fifth annual meeting of the Society for Psychotherapy Research, Denver, Co. (1974).

26. J. S. Maxmen, "Helping Patients Survive Our Theories: The Practice of an Educative Model." *Int. J. Group Psychother.* 34(1984):355–368.

27. Maxmen, "Helping Patients Survive Our Theories."

28. Rutan and Stone, *Psychodynamic Group Psychotherapy.*

29. Kellerman, H. *Group Psychotherapy and Personality: Intersecting Structures* (New York: Grune & Stratton, 1979), pp. 12–14.

6

Leading an Inpatient Psychotherapy Group

To lead usually implies to be in front, to guide, to persuade, to direct, to conduct while others follow. On inpatient units, group therapists frequently do lead in that manner – they are often responsible for patient privileges and restrictions, they sometimes prescribe medications, they carry out limit-setting functions, and they are responsible for patient safety. Furthermore, in the dependency culture of an inpatient ward, patients frequently *perceive* therapists as leading therapy groups in that manner.[1]

Although there are times in the group when therapists must lead in those ways to set limits or otherwise establish group safety,* in general therapists facilitate rather than "lead." The goal of their leadership is to facilitate the healing capacities of the group and its members. In fulfilling this task, therapists are actually more *followers* than leaders in that they follow the lead of the group rather than marching ahead of it. The direction of the group is determined by the needs of the members and not those of the therapist. A primary therapeutic tool for a dynamic psychotherapist is the *process* of the therapeutic material. To maximize the effectiveness of this tool, it is important that the therapist allow the natural group process to occur.

In fulfilling the role of leader/facilitator, the primary functions of

---

* See Chapter 8.

group therapists include establishing and maintaining the group therapy ground rules, or contract, listening to and observing the communications of the members and of themselves, and on that basis of listening and observing, to intervene in ways that facilitate the functioning of the group and the healing of its members.

In this chapter we examine those group leadership functions, and in the next chapter we examine the therapist's role in relation to specific kinds of patients and groups that may present particular difficulties.

ESTABLISHING AND MAINTAINING THE GROUP CONTRACT (The "Inside Contract")

Patients should agree to a specific group contract as a precondition to their being members. Establishing the ground rules for group therapy is the first task in leading any therapy group. The contract has additional significance in a hospital setting because of the complexity of the group context and the variety of roles and relationships between and among leaders and group members.

Within the group itself, the primary purpose of the contract is to provide a context in which effective therapy can take place. It makes possible the building of effective working alliances among the members and between the members and the therapist. We refer to this aspect of the contract as the "inside contract," in contrast with the "outside contract" described in Chapter 5, which deals primarily with the relationship of the group to the other parts of the hospital.

A MODEL (INSIDE) CONTRACT

The major features of the inside contract[2-4] of a psychodynamic inpatient therapy group are as follows:

1. Members agree to attend each session, be on time, and stay for the full session.
2. Members agree *not* to discuss information revealed in group sessions by other group members with patients who are not in the group.
3. Members agree to bring to the group any discussion of the group that may take place among them between group sessions, including the feelings generated by such contact.
4. Members agree to communicate by talking.

DISCUSSION OF THE CONTRACT

1. The agreement to attend each session and to stay for the entire meeting is a cornerstone of group therapy. It is certainly not expected that all the members of inpatient groups will be able to abide by the agreement, but it is important that they have made the agreement. This places the issue of mutual interdependence and responsibility directly into the arena of group discussion and observation, because the absence or lateness of a single member has an important effect on the entire group. This also has important implications for the establishing of, and testing of, basic trust. In other words, in trying to negotiate this fundamental agreement, members are confronted with some of the most difficult and important aspects of themselves. For inpatients, these are often issues highly related to the causes of hospitalization.

This also helps the patients struggle with motivation and with the place of group therapy within the hospital at large. For example, if a member makes individual therapy appointments that clash with the group therapy sessions the patient should be asked to reschedule the individual appointments. This decision is not based on the primacy of group therapy over other treatment modes, but on the simple fact that individual appointments are much easier to reschedule than a whole group. It is also based on the premise that maintenance of the group contract is an important ingredient in providing adequate treatment.

Where appropriate, the patient should be helped to understand any possible meaning in the scheduling conflict. Ideally, once the patient understands why the scheduling clash arose he or she will reschedule it without any directive. Clearly, such an intervention must take into consideration the capacity of the patient to address the issue and the fact that the patient may not have been given much choice about the schedule change. For many patients a simple directive is the most effective. In the meantime, the struggle with competing loyalties can yield important therapeutic gains.

2. The agreement to treat the information gained in group therapy with respect is also important if members are going to feel safe enough to reveal any significant information or emotion in the group meetings. Confidentiality in its purest sense is neither possible nor desirable on a hospital unit. Patients talk to each other in many settings and share their concerns with numbers of different people, both staff and patients. Additionally, staff must be able to communicate with each other about patients if they are to provide good treatment.

The manner in which group information is handled, however, is very important. All information should be handled with respect for the persons to whom it applies. To establish trust among group members and between the members and the therapist it is essential that the members know that the information they reveal is handled judiciously.

If some members wish to reveal things about themselves with others outside the group as well as inside it, that is their prerogative; but it is not their prerogative to give information about other group members outside the group.

When this contract is broken, as it inevitably will be on occasion, it must be discussed openly in the group. Such discussions, although sometimes quite painful, reinforce the degree of trust and respect among members. When the infringements are not discussed in the group, trust becomes difficult to maintain.

Discussion of these matters, which often extends into the community meetings as well, enables the patients to grapple with the limits of confidentiality and the role of responsibility. Several of the more common topics are: "If Joe tells me he is thinking of suicide, should I tell others and whom should I tell?" Another one is, "If I know my best friend is selling drugs on the unit and making some patients' drug problems worse, should I tell?"

3. The agreement to openly discuss in the group all matters that relate to the group or the relationships between group members, reinforces the notion that people can discuss things face to face and profit from that interaction. This, then, reinforces the fundamental maxim that even very private things can helpfully be spoken of with others, and further, that communicating about these matters ultimately helps rather than hurts all concerned.

4. The agreement to communicate with words rather than actions, although very important in all groups, is perhaps especially so in inpatient settings where some patients may have great difficulties with impulse control. Touching others in either affection or hostility, physically hurting oneself or others, or damaging property must be discouraged, and attempts at such behavior should be examined by the group to understand both the causes and the results of such behavior.

It is also important that therapists help members distinguish between honest expressions of angry emotions and sadistic verbalizations designed solely to cause pain. Most patients have no difficulty understanding the

limits placed on physical violence and are usually very relieved about it.
Verbal violence is not so easy to understand, particularly in an inpatient
setting. For many inpatients there is confusion between thinking angry
thoughts, feeling angry, expressing anger, and verbally assaulting someone else. For some the line between verbal expressions of anger and
physical violence is also a very thin one. For these reasons, some patients
are unable to give expression to any form of anger, no matter how mild,
for fear it may lead to a devastating outcome. It also makes it very
difficult for them to tolerate anger in others. Other patients, however,
will readily assault people without being aware of it, believing instead
that they are merely saying how angry they are.

The stress on verbal exchange also includes the agreement to honestly attempt to communicate with the others. Some therapists attempt
to legislate that all members of groups agree to use their "fair share" of
the group time. However, this is a very difficult concept because who is
to say what is fair for each member? Furthermore, silence can be a very
powerful communication, and group therapists should be willing to hear
and learn from the great differences in communicative style rather than
attempt to force all members to participate "equally."

CONCLUSION

The contract described above represents an ideal, and certain aspects of it are more abstract than some inpatients could grasp or exercise.
Hence, in applying the contract to their groups, therapists must use clinical judgment to determine how much of the contract the members can
reasonably be expected to understand and how much of it they are capable
of fulfilling. In most cases, however, even the most primitive patients
are capable of benefiting from a more thorough contract than many therapists believe. There is more danger in underestimating the interpersonal
capacities of inpatients than in overestimating them.

In initial interviews with potential level I group members, it is often
sufficient to let them know the time and place of the group and that they
are expected to attend, and leave other aspects of the contract to be dealt
with later as the need arises.

EXAMPLE. *A young, very frightened schizophrenic patient joined a level
I group. He said little in the group, and often looked distractedly at the*

> *floor. Occasionally he would lift his head and look at other members. After a number of sessions he began to make more direct contact with other members by getting up from his seat and poking a member with his finger. Although this was usually done gently, it was nevertheless experienced by the other members as quite intrusive.*
>
> *The therapists responded to the patient by acknowledging his wish to make contact with the others, but told him that the group rules precluded touching other people. They then suggested that he try to say something to the other members instead.*

This example indicates how therapists should always first attempt to understand all group behavior as attempts to communicate. Furthermore, it can be presumed that most communication of this sort has to do with the interpersonal wishes of the patient involved. The stress on verbal behavior rather than physical behavior is important in psychodynamic groups because it helps patients distinguish between feeling and doing, and because it helps them gain mastery of the very important interpersonal task of verbal communication. In other types of groups, such as dance or movement therapy, action takes priority over words. It is not that one is inherently better or more powerful than the other, only that different modalities require that one be primary to be most effective.

On rare occasions, patients' incapacity or unwillingness to understand and abide by the contract may necessitate more forceful measures.

> EXAMPLE. *A very angry, tall man entered a group with a walking cane. He placed a chair in the center of the group and sat down. He then began to rail at the group members and leader while turning round in his chair with his cane held out menacingly in front of him. Because of his height, there were few parts of the group or room that were beyond his reach.*
>
> *The group leader asked him to stop and sit with everyone else. He refused. The group leader immediately asked him to leave the group, which he did in a fit of rage.*

Needless to say, this event created considerable anxiety within the group and was the major topic for the rest of the session. In asking the patient to leave, however, the therapist was once again reinforcing aspects of the contract described above. He made it clear that threatening or dangerous behavior would not be tolerated. He was also making good on his agreement to provide a safe environment for the group members.

In summary, the contract provides the envelope[5] within which group therapy can take place. In communicating and maintaining the contract, it is important that therapists continually make it relevant to the issues that patients bring with them.

LISTENING TO THE PATIENTS

One of the central tasks of psychodynamic therapists is that of listening. Indeed, much of psychodynamic theory has emerged from the careful listening of many clinicians to many patients for almost a century.[6] Freud built his theory of personality on the basis of what he heard from his patients, and from that time until now careful listening has been the touchstone of dynamic therapists. This is not only true of theory building, it is also true for therapy practice. What therapists hear or do *not* hear determines the interventions they make.

How therapists listen is a complex process by which they seek to attain "a subjective grasp of the private experience of another person" (or persons) "based on careful and empathic observation of that person's words and actions."[7]

"Careful and empathic observation" means, among other things, being able to see the world from the patient's perspective while maintaining one's own perspective. To listen in this way also means being aware of the variety of ways in which patients communicate and the different levels at which those communications take place. Another complicating factor in the listening process is that what is communicated is filtered through the subjective experience of the listening therapist, with all the potential for editing and distortion that involves.

The process is especially complex in a group, where there are a number of persons in fairly constant interaction; and it is magnified even further in an inpatient setting where patients' language and behavior are sometimes bizarre and whose experience is often very different from that of most therapists. Under these circumstances, attaining a "subjective grasp" of even one patient's private experience may seem impossible, never mind that of six or eight patients. Furthermore, inpatient therapists must make their observations within severe time constraints. Those time constraints are created by the limited capacity of the patients to tolerate the thoughtful consideration of their experience, on the one hand, and by the brevity of most hospital stays on the other. Inpatient therapists often do not have the luxury of waiting for long periods of time to see and hear what processes or issues emerge in their groups. On the other hand, because of the oppressive and painful material that inpatients are burdened with, there may be times when each group seems endless, no matter how long or short the actual time available. *All* inpatient group therapists feel confused and overwhelmed by the content, or lack of it, during some group sessions.

Given these particular difficulties it is not surprising that inpatient therapists frequently bypass the listening process and seek instead particular techniques to facilitate their work. "What topics should we talk about?" "Are there useful exercises to help people talk?" "What can we do to help our patients talk about anger or control their anger?" "Should we plan topics in advance?" These questions, however understandable, often reflect therapists' anxieties and frustrations in working with difficult patients rather than a reflection of patient needs.

Though listening in inpatient therapy groups may have special difficulties, it is still a central task for the therapists and essential to making effective interventions. The material that follows describes ways by which therapists can listen to the sometimes confusing and frightening material that arises in inpatient groups and begin to "hear" and understand the communications the members are making.

WAYS TO FACILITATE LISTENING

There are eight sources of data that inpatient group therapists can use to facilitate their task of listening to group members. They are:

1. Events on the unit floor
2. Group's history
3. Group's developmental phase
4. Group content
5. Group process
6. Individual patient's history
7. Knowledge of the developmental level of patients' communications
8. Therapists' Affective Responses
   a. Reality-based therapist responses
   b. Countertransference responses

By using these sources, therapists strengthen the accuracy with which they can hear the needs of the individual members and of the groups as a whole. They can provide therapists with a knowledge of the adaptive tasks of the members and clues to the nature of the members' affective and adaptive responses to those tasks.

DISCUSSION OF WAYS TO FACILITATE LISTENING

Events on the Unit Floor. A primary tenet of dynamic theory is that behavior is not random, but rather is meaningful and connected to events and affects in the life of the individual. Because a powerful stimulus in the lives of all inpatients is the activity on the unit floor, knowing what is happening on the floor makes it easier for therapists to hear what is happening in their groups. If group therapists are not working on the floor, it is helpful to check with the floor staff about events on the unit before beginning a group session.

> EXAMPLE. *A group therapist arrived for his first group of the day. When he entered his office he was surprised to find one patient lying in the middle of the floor, another curled up in a heap on an arm chair, another hyperventilating, another crying uncontrollably, and yet another complaining in a loud voice about her boyfriend in prison. The remaining patients were quiet and frightened.*
>
> *The group leader was puzzled and rather anxious – nothing made sense. His co-therapist who had arrived a few moments ahead of him began assisting the patient who was hyperventilating by getting her to breathe into a brown paper bag. He joined her and asked, "What's been going on?" The co-therapist who worked on the floor told the following story.*
>
> *An adolescent patient had disappeared on the hospital grounds and the police were called. Shortly after they arrived a young, inexperienced police officer saw the youth running into the trees. Whereupon the officer drew his gun from his holster and fired several shots into the air.*
>
> *The two leaders then sat down and said to the group members, "Let's talk about this irresponsible and frightening shooting that took place on the hospital grounds this morning." Slowly the group members began to calm down and talk about the event, and about the terror, disappointment, and rage they felt not only toward the police officer, but also toward the staff for failing to protect them.*

Until the male therapist knew about the events on the floor the bizarre behavior (communication) of the members made no sense to him and he did not know how to intervene. Once the adaptive context was known, however, the unusual behavior could be understood. The therapists were then able to open the matter up for discussion, rather than allow it to continue to be avoided through regressive behavior, and this enabled the members to relate the event to their affective experience and to bear it.

Group's History.   Knowledge of what happened in previous group sessions or earlier in the same session can be helpful in understanding the communications and behaviors of group members.

> EXAMPLE. *As a therapist enters her group the members are busily talking to each other in a friendly manner. No one acknowledges her arrival. The pace of the conversation gradually slows, but the members continue to ignore her. This is unusual behavior for this group. As the therapist listens, she notes to herself that she had been out of the hospital for a week, and that another therapist had led the group for her. From this she hypothesized that the group's behavior was probably related to those aspects of the group's recent history. After hearing a number of other comments from members that suggested her hypothesis was accurate she said the group seemed reluctant to welcome her back. The conversation stopped; one member glared at her and said, "I wish you hadn't come back! The man who led when you were away was so much better. He was warm and kind. He cared about us. He wasn't cold like you are." Others joined, talking about how much better the group had been in her absence.*

In this example recognition of the recent events in the group enabled the therapist to recognize the group's adaptive task and help the members address it. This particular event is fairly common in inpatient settings, particularly during the holiday seasons. Yet, it is surprising how often it can be overlooked. Sometimes in the activity of an acute unit we overlook the impact of missing a few group sessions.

Group's Developmental Phase.   Another piece of data that can facilitate the process of listening for therapists is knowledge of group development. Earlier (Chapter 3) we noted that an inpatient therapy group is a living organism that changes over time. There is an early bonding phase, when the members are getting to know each other, a reactive phase when members emphasize their differences and protest the rules, a mature phase when a variety of issues are dealt with, and an ending phase when some of the group members are leaving, and so on. This particular rhythm can also be seen in an individual session.

Those phases also represent fairly discrete adaptive tasks for the group members. Saying "hello" is a specific task that differs from saying "good-bye." Thus the same words and behaviors mean different things during different phases and require different interventions by the therapist. The members of group A and group B, for instance, may both seem somewhat withdrawn and hesitant about participating. Both groups may talk about the difficulties of dealing with change and may share other common themes, but their adaptive tasks may be quite different because the groups are in different developmental phases. Group A may have had three or four new members added that session and the members are struggling with saying hello, whereas group B may be in the mature phase in which the members are dealing with the changes and losses that being in the hospital has wrought on their lives.

The specific comments of individual members will also be heard differently and responded to differently in each group. If patient B in group B talks about a number of very personal aspects of himself, the therapist will probably hear that as a wish to reveal himself to his peers and gain help with some issues related to his difficulty with change. The therapist or other group members may even point out ways in which his behavior in the group has made it difficult for him to deal effectively with change.

By contrast if patient A in group A began sharing the same kind of personal matters as patient B it would be heard as patient A's way of saying "hello," and *not* as an invitation for further exploration by the therapist and other members. To explore further would be like undressing the patient while the rest of the members remained fully clothed. It would also be a way of making patient A a scapegoat, which in turn may be how this patient historically says "hello" by taking on the negative feelings for the group. The therapist's intervention would be to help the group understand that all the various behaviors in this early meeting of a group are different ways members say hello and to otherwise facilitate the bonding process.

Group Content (Overt and Covert).   Group content refers to the things that members say and do. Listening to group content is sometimes very straightforward. Members give information about themselves or comment about events in language that is clear and easy to understand. For instance, a patient arrives a few minutes late for the group and says, "The nurse who was giving me my medication was running a few minutes late." That statement is clear and is often best accepted and understood in the manner in which it is given. The therapist may merely say, "Thanks for letting us know, I'm glad you were able to make it anyway."

Human language is highly symbolic, however, and even the most straightforward of statements may be laden with meanings other than those immediately apparent. This is readily demonstrated in everyday speech, in writing, in poetry, and in love songs where words are often understood to carry larger meanings than their literal meaning. If I say, for instance, "I'm straining at the leash" most people will understand that I am describing a strong wish to be free, or get started on a venture, task, or whatever. The statement is unlikely to be understood literally.

There are times, however, when we may use words or behavior symbolically without being aware that we are doing it. One of Freud's great discoveries was that people will often communicate about themselves and particularly about their unconscious or preconscious wishes and conflicts without being aware of it. If during an individual therapy session, for instance, a man says "I'm straining at the leash," he may discover, when he follows his associations, that he is struggling to be free from some attachment to or dependency on the therapist that is causing him a great deal of anxiety. He may also discover that he has been dealing with the same struggle with some central figures from early in life and didn't know it. Hence the phrase "I'm straining at the leash" when used in this particular symbolic way – having unconscious or preconscious meaning as well as conscious meaning – would be viewed as a derivative of the patient's unconscious or preconscious concerns.

Patients do the same thing in groups. Members will often convey to each other and to the therapists the nature of their unconscious or preconscious concerns through the use of derivative material. Thus as therapists listen to their groups they can make inferences from the content and behavior in the group about possible group and individual concerns that may lie outside the members' awareness.

> EXAMPLE. *Members of a group began the session by talking about Catholic priests who do not abide by the ten commandments. They debated at length about which priests broke what commandments and how they should be treated. They also debated about the poor treatment of the student nurses on the floor by other staff. The leaders tried to make a number of interventions but found that most of what they said fell on deaf ears. Although the group seemed to run quite well and the members engaged in enthusiastic and animated conversation, the leaders remained confused about the session. They never felt a part of it and noted that the group members had avoided working directly on their psychological concerns.*
>
> *At a staff meeting following the session it was suggested to the leaders that the talk about priests who break the ten commandments may have been an indirect (derivative) communication of the members' anger at the leaders for having broken the group rules. One of the leaders, they noted, had missed the group for several weeks because of surgery, and the other leader had missed one session recently and had arrived late at this one.*

The talk about the nurses, they suggested, may also have been an indirect expression of how they felt they were being treated.

At the next session those hypotheses were confirmed. The members again communicated their concerns in indirect ways, but this time the leaders were able to hear it. After several brief interventions they enabled the members to talk about how upset they were at the leaders' absences, a fact they had been unable to acknowledge either to themselves or to the therapists up to that point.

Group Process. Group process refers to the sequence of verbal and nonverbal interactions that take place between the members of the group, the flow from one topic to the next, the movement from periods of talking to periods of silence, from periods of activity to periods of inactivity, and so on. This process can be understood as analogous to free association in psychoanalysis. Just as in that case, it is presumed that conversation is rarely disconnected from what went before, and that important information about the unconscious concerns of a group can be derived by careful examination of the process.

The consultation that the staff gave to the therapists in our last example was possible because they also knew the group process as well as the group content and the recent events in the therapists' lives. The patients' initial concern about the behavior of priests is open to as many interpretations as one's imagination may wish to create. But when content is heard as part of the group process its meaning for the group and its members becomes clearer. Listening to the process helps therapists determine if a particular content is a response to a therapist intervention, events in earlier sessions, a particular member's ongoing concerns, a current interaction between certain members or some future event such as a discharge from the hospital or a court hearing.

In our example the process went from discussion of priests breaking rules, to visiting parents who were ill and feeling tired about having to do it, to parents who did not come through, to anger at the bad treatment student nurses received in the hospital, to concern about violence in an unsafe world. These topics flowed readily from one to the next, and most patients took part. There were fewer silent patients than usual and everyone seemed highly engaged by the topics. But the therapists felt excluded and their interventions were largely ignored. Thus even if the staff had not known about the recent events in the therapists' lives they could infer with some confidence that the group members had some anxiety and anger about the leaders' behavior and their own responses to it.

Individual Patient's History.   Though we are dedicated to the use of groups in helping people in psychological distress, we never lose sight of the fact that the individual patient is our primary concern. Many times a therapist cannot fully understand the meanings of a particular group session without reference to the specific individuals who comprise the group. It is often difficult for group therapists to gain and keep in mind the histories of each of the patients in their groups, but it is important that they do so. Though groups help their members recognize that they are part of the human condition and that many of their problems are universal, nonetheless the goal of psychodynamic therapy is to ultimately assist individuals in understanding how their lives are unique. Each individual perceives life according to the particulars of his or her history. What for one would be a minor aggravation, for another might be an extremely traumatic event.

> EXAMPLE. *Dr. Oliver, a psychiatric resident, was finishing his residency and consequently leaving as group therapist. In his final meeting, the patients had various reactions to his departure. To cite just two: Mavis was grateful to Dr. Oliver for the help she had received from him, and she brought him some flowers she had picked on the hospital grounds. Orrin sat mutely throughout the meeting, never making eye contact with Dr. Oliver.*
>
> *After that meeting two significant events occurred. First, Orrin disappeared from the hospital. Second Dr. Oliver developed a severe case of poison ivy.*

Information from the history of these two patients sheds light on these events. Orrin's life had taken a dramatic turn for the worse when he was eleven, at which time his father left for another woman. Orrin's mother was devastated by this event and turned her rage to Orrin, whom she beat unmercifully. He finally ran away from home and lived on the streets for two years. Mavis also came from a broken home, but in her case the mother remarried within months of the divorce. Mavis seemingly turned all her love to her stepfather and was very open about her love for this man who "saved my life." During her adolescence, however, she engaged in a series of behaviors that seriously stressed the relationship with her stepfather, including wrecking his brand new Mercedes, breaking a treasured antique that had been in his family for generations, and burning a hole in one of his expensive silk shirts while attempting to iron it.

Had Dr. Oliver known or remembered the histories of Mavis and Orrin, he might have been able to help them explore more fully the symbolic meaning of his leaving. Mavis had denied the anguish she felt over her father's departure and overidealized her stepfather. The repressed anger and hurt was evident in the series of "accidents" that caused her stepfather discomfort. Similarly, under the guise of warmth and pure gratitude, her gift of flowers "accidentally" included some poison ivy. This is not to imply that she did not feel warmly or grateful to Dr. Oliver. He *had* been helpful to her and she did feel very warmly toward him. But, as with her stepfather, there were ambivalent feelings and she did not allow herself access to the negative feelings.

Orrin's behavior was also understandable in light of his history. When he lost his father he ultimately had to run away to protect himself. Though he gave no verbal evidence that he was similarly affected by Dr. Oliver's departure, he subsequently used the same defense. Had Dr. Oliver recalled Orrin's history and attempted to help him express his reactions to the termination, he might have been able to forestall the subsequent running away.

Many of the examples throughout this text indicate the importance of individual histories in fully understanding the responses of members. Given the brevity of many patients' stay on inpatient units, along with the demands made on staff members' time for many tasks on the unit, it is easy for group therapists to avoid getting the specific histories of the members of their groups. But this results in significant opportunities for learning being lost.

Knowledge of the Developmental Level of Patients' Communications. In listening to the members of our groups it is important to be aware of the developmental level from which they are communicating. Hedges[8] notes that many of the differences that have emerged in psychoanalytic theory have developed because the theorists were listening to patients whose concerns sprang from different levels of emotional development. If a person is healthy or neurotic, one often hears of concerns about guilt and conflict around sex and aggression, much as Freud heard. By contrast, if a patient is psychotic one is more liable to hear terror about disintegration and annihilation, or fear of merger and loss of self if borderline.

> EXAMPLE. *A therapist found himself intensely drawn toward Maude, an attractive young woman in his group. That he found her attractive seemed reasonable enough, but the intensity of the attraction puzzled him. She had just joined the group and he knew little about her. After the group*

session he spoke to the head nurse about her. The head nurse's response to the patient was equally intense, but complementary to the therapist's. She became easily enraged at her for no apparent reason. Other staff reacted with similar intense reactions as the therapist and head nurse. As the therapist thought about this information he hypothesized that this attractive young woman related to people either by merging with them and idealizing them, or by distancing them and denigrating them. That is, she split people into good and bad objects.

The next group session was slow moving and somewhat boring. At the end of the session Maude spoke in a very pleasant and coy manner to the therapist. She told him how wonderful a therapist he was. She then noted that the group had been very dull. She had wanted to talk about a number of important matters and knew the therapist could have helped her, but she knew the other group members would have found it too difficult because they seemed to be at a different place from her. Then she asked if the therapist could see his way to putting her in another of his groups that was better suited to her.

At face value her request seemed reasonable. The group was indeed dull and the other members seemed to pale beside her. But the therapist decided to make no changes and asked her to bring the matter up at the next group session. She did not want to wait until then. The stay in the hospital was so short she could not afford to waste any time in bad groups, she said. The atmosphere had changed. She left the room enraged. The therapist no longer felt intensely drawn toward her. His feelings were closer to those of the head nurse.

At the next session Maude was still angry and said she wanted to leave the group and go to another one. Other members pleaded on her behalf. "Why shouldn't she go? After all people have a right to make their own choices." After some angry debate the leader intervened. He said that some group sessions were indeed more difficult than others and very uncomfortable to be in. But that could be talked about. He was not going to make any transfers. Maude was momentarily furious, then she settled down and the group proceeded. The leader no longer felt intensely drawn toward her or enraged at her.

The therapist heard Maude's communications as coming from someone whose development was arrested at, or had regressed to, that of the separation–individuation phase of development. She was not able to integrate "bad" and "good" objects. People were either all good (the therapist) or all bad (the head nurse). She also often yearned for intense and immediate intimacy with an all good object, on the one hand, but dreaded it, on the other, because her sense of identity was threatened by such intimacy. Consequently an all good person (the therapist) could readily become an all bad person, as a way of making a break from a threatening intimacy. Because he was listening at this level, the therapist choose to remain firm, but available (not seduced into an overly close relationship or driven away by sending the patient to another group) and to allow the patient to determine for herself what was a comfortable distance. In this instance the therapist was much like the mother who remains constant as the child moves back and forth from her both physically and emotionally during the separation–individuation phase of development.

During the group various members had argued that it was a person's right to choose which group was best for them. We have heard this argument often in inpatient groups, and it is not without merit. Clearly, the group was in a protest phase and one might hear Maude's wishes as a healthy person in conflict about the limits of her rights and responsibilities, and how she could best assert herself in this group. If Maude had been heard at this level then the therapist and the group may have begun to explore with her why she wished to assert herself by leaving rather than deal directly with the therapist. Valuable as such an approach may be with a neurotic patient, or with Maude later in treatment, it would most likely have intensified her involvement with the therapist at this time and increased her terror and rage rather than reduce it.

Knowing the developmental level from which patients' communications are being made enables therapists to hear and respond in ways that are appropriate to patients' needs.

Therapists' Affective Responses. As well as listening to data from group members and from the group environment, it is also important that therapists listen to themselves and to their responses to group events. The responses of group therapists may be classed into two broad categories: therapists' responses that are reality based and countertransference responses.

Reality-Based Therapist Responses. These are the most straightforward of therapists' responses. The human dramas that are talked about and experienced in therapy groups touch all of us. Thus, if a group therapist experiences sadness that is not related to his own personal life while listening to a group, it is very likely that the group members are also feeling sad. Sometimes the congruence between the therapist's feelings and those of the members is very obvious. The members may be talking about recent losses in the group and in their personal lives so that it is not very surprising that the therapist is feeling sad.

Sometimes, however, the congruence between the therapist's affect and the group's behavior is not always that obvious. When that is the case it becomes particularly important for therapists to listen to themselves.

> EXAMPLE. *A group was meeting for its second session of the week. The members were very happy and joked a great deal. Most, including the therapist, found the atmosphere to be very enjoyable. After a period of time, however, the therapist felt sad and was puzzled by the incongruence between his feelings and the overt behavior of the members. He listened for some time and noted to himself that the members were joking about some pretty sad things. He also noticed that several members had remained quiet throughout most of the session. Suspecting that they may be carrying some of the split off affect that he was experiencing, he asked how the group was for them. One member pouted and said little, whereas another said "I don't know what everyone finds so funny," and talked about how sad she was feeling about the loss of her roommate. The mood of the group changed. Other members then talked about some patients who had been recently discharged before they thought they were ready and how badly they felt about that.*

The incongruence, as is often the case, had turned out to be more apparent than real. The therapist's sadness turned out to be congruent with the groups' real affect that was being defended against by the laughter and the jokes.

Countertransference Responses. Countertransference takes place when therapists' responses to their group members are generated, in whole or in part, by repressed thoughts, feelings, fantasies, and conflicts related to significant persons and experiences in their own pasts. Those responses can often get in the way of effective listening and the interventions that ensue can hinder the group process. When they are acknowledged and understood, however, the interference can be reduced and at times turned into an asset.

> EXAMPLE. *Mark, a nurse's aide, ran into a series of difficulties with patients, both in a group and on the floor. He was often angry with patients and they with him. He was aware of the patients' anger at him, but not*

of his anger at them. During a group supervision session the following emerged.

While working on the floor, he was often the member of the nursing staff who set limits on patient behavior. When patients became overly rowdy he would quiet them down. He resented this task for two reasons. First, the other staff members seemed unwilling to do it, and second, when he did it, he often ended up in an angry struggle with the patients. He then felt blamed by the staff for the conflicts that ensued.

Further discussion with his peers revealed that he was not able to tolerate as high a level of noise among the patients as they were. When the patients became a little rowdy he was the first to make a move to bring it to an end. Furthermore, other staff members knew there were times when it was helpful to turn a deaf ear to the noise because it merely signaled good spirits, at other times they knew a brief comment with a touch of humor would be sufficient, whereas at other times they had to be more firm. For Mark all infractions were addressed very seriously. His peers also noted that when he did set limits he often sounded very angry even though he spoke in an even tone. This surprised Mark because he was not aware of being angry.

At a later staff meeting Mark revealed that his parents had been in a concentration camp during World War II. They survived and came to live in the States. The matter was rarely mentioned in his family, but Mark was always aware of what he termed "a great silence" that weighed heavily. A message he picked up from this great silence was that he should be serious minded, do well, and cause as little trouble as possible. Rowdiness among the patients stirred up for him his own wish to rebel against the "great silence" and so it had to be calmed as soon as possible. Mark realized that this would be an ongoing concern for him, but acknowledging its presence enabled him to relax somewhat on the floor and in the group.

Mark's countertransference responses had led to interventions that interfered with the group process, caused unnecessary conflict, and reduced the level of trust. When he became aware of his countertransference responses he was able to reduce their impact.

There is another side to Mark's countertransference. Because of Mark's history he was particularly sensitive to times in the group when important issues were hidden behind silences. Thus Mark's knowledge of himself and of his own conflicts not only reduced interference, but he was also able to use that knowledge to turn his particular sensitivity into an asset.

Projective Identification.   Mark's countertransference responses were unique to him. They were rooted in his special history and his particular responses to that history. There are, however, some universal countertransference responses. For instance, a therapist may meet with a patient and react with revulsion, or feel enraged or very anxious and have difficulty responding helpfully to the patient. When the therapist checks this out with colleagues he or she may discover that they react in a similar or complementary way to the same patient. The countertransferential responses may be uniquely colored by each clinician, but the experiences are basically the same. Those universal countertransferences are generated when therapists become the receivers of patients' projective identifications.†

Difficult as those reactions may be to cope with, universal countertransferences are additional pieces of information that, when discerned, can help therapists better understand their patients and their groups.

By examining the floor-wide reactions to Maude, in our earlier example,‡ the therapist was able to realize that part of Maude's interpersonal style was to generate intense and passionate responses in all who encounter her. This capacity, both an asset and a liability in terms of her capacity to gain and sustain intimacy, had to be understood as part of her self-protection in her new role as hospitalized patient.

Clearly, these sources of data are interrelated and most experienced therapists move back and forth between them as they listen to their groups. Often they may listen to numbers of them at the same time. The beginning therapist may find such a list intimidating and like a beginning musician may have to listen to the notes one at a time. But with practice and good supervision, the beginning therapist will find that the notes begin to come together and the music becomes clearer.

INTERVENTIONS

The interventions that therapists make are the result of what they listen to and hear. When discussing listening in the previous section we included some instances of therapists' interventions that grew out of what they heard. In this section we focus on some specific and fairly gener-

---

† For more detailed discussion of projective identification, see Chapter 2.
‡ See pp. 113–114.

alizable interventions the use and timing of which are based on careful listening. We discuss:

1. Level of therapist activity and frequency of interventions
2. Here-and-now versus there-and-then interventions
3. Beginning the group, facilitating bonding, and encouraging interactions
4. "Round the room" interventions
5. Interventions around metaphors
6. Conferring meaning

Level of Therapist Activity.   There is a widely accepted axiom that therapists should be more active when leading an inpatient group than when leading an outpatient group. Although this is often true in practice it is open to abuse if the rationale for that axiom is not understood. Therapists are usually, though not always, more active when leading inpatient groups because the members of inpatient groups usually are less able to tolerate the anxiety generated by the group experience than members of outpatient groups.

Therapists are silent during a group session to allow the group interactions to develop freely and the process of the group to flow relatively uninhibited. When that happens the members' concerns readily surface and who they are as persons – their strengths and weaknesses, including the liabilities that brought them to the hospital in the first place – becomes clear and available for understanding and change. The healing value of the group process is allowed to develop.

For some patients, however, the relative lack of structure that is created by the leader's silence increases their anxiety to a point where they feel unsafe and are unable to function effectively. Rather than create a group structure of their own in response to the leader's inactivity, these members regress in unhelpful ways and the group may become severely fragmented. This is most likely to happen with patients who lack stable internal structures of their own, or whose internal structures have been rendered ineffective by an overwhelming crisis. These conditions are more likely to be found among members of an inpatient population than among outpatients.

The activity level of group therapists, then, must be such as to permit member interactions and group process to take place freely, on the one hand, without leading to iatrogenic anxiety among the members on the other. As a rule, when members are interacting freely, even intensely, therapists intervene only occasionally, and usually in ways that facilitate the interactive process further or help the members better understand themselves and their roles in that process. When the level of anxiety reaches nonproductive levels therapists must then intervene more often, at times firmly and with directives about inappropriate behavior. To not intervene when members are in such distress would be cruel and antitherapeutic. It can also be antitherapeutic, however, to underestimate the capacity of our patients to tolerate moderate levels of anxiety in a group and to allow our activity to overwhelm the process and infantilize the members.

In summary, because members of inpatient groups have less capacity to organize themselves and their environment than members of outpatient groups, therapists are usually more active when leading inpatient groups than when leading outpatient groups. For the same reason, therapists are usually more active when leading level I inpatient groups than when leading level II groups.

Here-and-Now Versus There-and-Then Interventions.   Here-and-now interventions address the members' current interactions and experiences in the group, in contrast with those interventions that address the historical roots of the members' behavior and experiences, the there-and-then interventions. There has been a great deal of controversy among therapists as to which interventions are more valuable. We believe that in most therapy situations therapists must deal with both the past and the present because they are so closely related. The here-and-now responses of people in therapy are often repetitions of earlier there-and-then experiences. Furthermore, the unconscious knows no time limits,[9] hence for the unconscious there is no past or future; all personal events are forever in the present. Transference always takes place in the present but its perceptions are from the past. The important task for therapists is to judge when it is helpful to focus on one or another of these two important facets of the same experience.

In inpatient groups we believe that it is best to use primarily here-and-now interventions. The level of distress in inpatients, particularly in the members of level I groups, is often so compelling that they have little capacity to look at the past. The pain of the present is front and center stage and needs to be addressed. If a group member is emotionally wounded during a group session, for instance, that injury must be dealt with before further therapy can take place. To suggest to the patient that his pain is due to the fact that he perceived and reacted to a particular member as though he were his father, mother, or sister will only add insult to injury. At some later time, when the patient is better reconstituted that intervention might prove very helpful, but not when the patient's emotional flesh is raw. Talking about the past when a patient is in acute distress is usually experienced by the patient as a failure in empathy and causes further injury. In addition, focusing prematurely on the past may also cause further regression in the patient rather than healing.

By contrast, focusing on the present helps establish a stronger empathic relationship with patients by recognizing the immediacy of their distress. It enables them to deal directly with that current distress, gain mastery of it, and begin the process of returning to, at least, a premorbid level of functioning.

From the perspective of the group-as-a-whole, it must be recognized that interpersonal connections must be made and trust and safety among members established before exploration of a person's past may begin. To begin such a venture earlier would, as we have noted before, risk making a scapegoat of the member and significantly increase the level of anxiety and mistrust in the group.

Although it is true that most interventions in inpatient groups should be here-and-now in focus, it must be acknowledged that there are rare occasions when therapists may use there-and-then interventions. They happen when one is leading a stable group of patients who have done very well in the hospital and are about to be discharged. Under these circumstances, patients will sometimes begin to make connections themselves. They will speak of how a particular patient or set of circumstances reminds them of a part of their past. They may also recognize that their behavior was more determined by that relationship or event than by the current one. When such connections between the present and the past arise in this spontaneous way, therapists can effectively reinforce them and encourage other members to think in a similar manner. This process strengthens the members' capacity to think psychologically and prepares them for long-term psychodynamic group psychotherapy when they leave.[10] In other words, if therapists listen effectively they will be alert to those rare occasions when connections between the past and the present can be effectively made.

Beginning the Group. Because of the rapid turnover of inpatient populations, each group session has some of the characteristics of a new group. Even when the hospital census is relatively stable, there is usually at least one new member in each session. For these reasons, therapists must pay careful attention to the beginning of the session and in particular to the welcoming of new members and the rebonding of the other members.

At the beginning, it is helpful for therapists to introduce themselves, giving their name and role in the hospital and in the group. For example, "I am Dr. X., a psychologist on the staff and the leader of this group." If there are any observers in the group they should also be mentioned and their role clarified. Therapists should then very briefly state the purpose and ground rules of the group. Lastly, new members should be introduced.

In some relatively stable groups where there may be only one new member, other members of the group may perform some of these tasks for the leader. Some may spontaneously introduce a new member, for instance, and the process of incorporating that new member may take place rapidly. The new member may already be well known and well liked on the floor so that the welcoming process may be quite brief and the group will move on to other issues.

By contrast in another group the new member may be well known but disliked on the floor. When new members are disliked, the other members will probably find ways to avoid welcoming them. It is important for therapists to be alert to this process and enable the members to talk about their discomfort.

During the welcoming process, disliked new members will often display why they are disliked by presenting themselves in angry, cold, disdainful, intrusive, or other unpleasant ways. When this happens therapists are sometimes tempted to "do therapy" with the unpleasant newcomers to make them fit the group better. Usually more is gained when therapists recognize that those unpleasant behaviors are the ways these patients cope with being new to the hospital and to the group. Therapists can then intervene by noting that "we all say hello in different ways, some of us jump in readily, whereas others prefer to keep a distance and may get angry if new people get close too quickly." Comments of this nature often help reduce the anxiety of new members, make sense of the experience for other members, and enable the group to move forward. Therapists should also be alert to the fact that sometimes new members are disliked simply because they are new, and not because of any particular unpleasant characteristics of their own.

When a large number of new members join the group the remaining members will sometimes feel overwhelmed. Rather than welcome the new members they may withdraw. This can sometimes be very discouraging to the beginning therapist, particularly if recent groups seem to have gone very well—not an unusual experience when a number of members have done well in the hospital and are about to be discharged. Rather than try to recreate the old successful group, however, therapists gain more if they address the changes that have just taken place in the group and encourage members to talk about being new, and about having lost "old" members and about welcoming new ones. Members will then feel freer to introduce themselves to each other and the group can begin to rebuild.

The primary tasks, then, of therapists at the beginning of a group are to introduce themselves, the observers, and other staff where applicable, outline the purpose and ground rules of the group, and introduce new members. Having made those introductions, therapists then facilitate the process of bonding that follows. Sometimes this may take only a brief portion of the session, as when a well-liked new member is added to a stable group, or it may be the major issue for a whole session or longer if, for example, the patient is disliked or if the group is accepting many new members and is essentially being rebuilt.

As well as facilitating the growth and stability of the group as a therapeutic organ, the process of beginning the group also performs an important therapeutic function for the members. It gives the members an opportunity to develop some skill in an area they often find difficult, namely, making connections with other people.

This is particularly true in level I groups where making connections with others is the central issue and where beginnings are a constant and recurring task for the leaders and the members. Often, in a level I group beginning the group is *the* issue for one session after another. For members of these groups, making connections with others is both a longed for and highly dreaded experience. We have often been amazed at how readily members of level I groups become attached to their groups and equally amazed at how disoriented they can become in the presence of their peers or how strongly they may avoid contact with specific members.

Beginning a level I group is thus a more difficult task than in a level II group and requires more active involvement by the therapist. Therapists beginning a level I group will introduce themselves much as we described earlier and the group may, on occasion, also follow the lines we described above. But often members of a level I group have considerable difficulty saying "hello" and introducing themselves. This is because members of these groups are sometimes unwilling or unable to recognize the other members as separate people. If a person gives their name other members may be too self-absorbed to remember it or to hear it clearly. Or members may introduce themselves as the Messiah or in other ways that make it difficult for members to respond. Some are just too terrified to speak. Lastly, members of level I groups sometimes have difficulty carrying the bonding made in one session over into the next.

To enable the members to say hello and maintain anxiety at a manageable level, therapists must become active mediators of communication. One useful way of doing this is to spend a significant amount of time on introductions. For instance, the therapists may ask the members to give their names and then, after each person gives his or her name, they check that everyone else in the group heard and understood what was said. In more severely regressed groups the leaders may ask for the names of the members in sequence and check that each person heard and is able to repeat the name of the person next to him or her and so on round the group.

Spending time on the introductions in this manner enables the members to recognize the existence of others in the group and to be recognized in turn. It also helps to reduce the dread of others and reinforces the natural desire to make contact.

While introducing themselves members will sometimes give additional information along with their names. When that happens therapists can actively weave that information into the introductions, and encourage others to add similar information. Therapists reward the contributions members make by acknowledging them and finding ways to include them in the group process. This is true even of contributions that may be inappropriate, as in the case of the schizophrenic patient who poked other patients. In that instance, the therapist recognized the patient's wish to make contact with other members and suggested other, more appropriate ways of doing it.

Those interventions help to weave a network of connections among the members. Initially, the connections run through the therapists who provide the initial "glue" for the group members. The therapists' goal, however, is to gradually step back and allow the members to make direct and safe verbal contact with each other with a modicum of trust. Occasionally, that may happen in one session, but there will be other times in level I groups when therapists may spend numbers of sessions being the group's "glue" and actively moderating the communications before the members feel safe about speaking directly to each other.

In summary, the therapists' interventions when beginning groups, whether level I or level II groups, are designed to build connections among the members, and establish an optimal level of trust (or reduce distrust to a manageable level) and safety.

"Round the Room" Interventions. Checking with the members of the group individually as in the beginning of a level I group can also be useful at other times in both level I and level II groups. Most therapists have led groups in which there is little response from the members. Sometimes this may be because the members are very upset about events on the floor or in the group and are afraid to speak or because they are expressing their anger by refusing to speak. When therapists are aware of the upsetting events they can often facilitate member interactions by mentioning the events and encouraging the members to talk about them. Once the unspeakable is spoken the members will feel freer to talk.

There are times, however, when such interventions have little impact. This can happen when group members are very depressed and isolated from one another and seem to lack the will to participate. At other times they may be just too anxious to respond to general statements. Under these kinds of circumstances, it can be helpful to make contact with the members individually. The therapist speaks briefly to one patient and then to another, sometimes in order around the room, until each patient is spoken to. What they speak about is determined by the task of the group, whether it is dealing with new members, loss of old members, or a specific event in the group. The round the room intervention can help reduce anxiety to tolerable levels or draw out members who feel unable to motivate themselves. In doing this, therapists will also often learn what it is the members are unable to talk about. Sometimes, the group members may begin to respond before the therapist has completed the round; at other times it may be several sessions before members feel able to talk easily. In either case once the group begins interacting the therapist can step back and be less active. When members have a particularly difficult time interacting, therapists should evaluate the membership balance of their groups and, when appropriate, add new members who can provide some complementary behavior and affect[11] to balance the overly passive or depressed weight of the current membership.

Interventions Around Metaphors. Words, statements, events, and numerous other things can become metaphors for the concerns, conflicts, and adaptive tasks of an individual or group of individuals large or small. Inpatients are particularly prone to use metaphors to describe their concerns. Sometimes those metaphors are so idiosyncratic and bizarre that little understanding of the patients' concerns can be gained. There are times, however, when with careful listening they can be understood and become a platform for useful interventions. Sometimes addressing the metaphor may mean saying and doing nothing, because through the metaphor the patient may be asking the therapist to remain quiet and maintain a respectful distance. At other times a more active response can be helpful.

> EXAMPLE. *Norm, a pleasant, but quite agitated patient, broke into the process of a smoothly running group by claiming that he had lost one of his blue birds. He claimed he had four blue birds, but one had disappeared. He was sure he would lose the rest. He spoke in an agitated and rambling manner. Other group members were puzzled and somewhat anxious. One member said, "Norm you never had any blue birds, you're crazy." But Norm insisted. The therapist felt as puzzled as the members. Norm's insistence on the importance of the blue birds and the fact that he had lost one seemed bizarre. By all accounts the blue birds were a figment of Norm's imagination. But for Norm they were not imagined, they were real. As the therapist listened he realized that a very well liked and highly respected member of the group named Joan had left the hospital since the last session. He also realized that Norm sat very close to Joan in the group and considered her his special friend. She, along with several other women, had helped Norm get to group sessions when he was afraid to be there. So the therapist turned to Norm and asked. "Is Joan the blue bird you are missing? She left the hospital yesterday and she was very important to you." Norm stopped protesting and after a pause that seemed to go on forever shook his head up and down. Norm no longer acted strangely and along with the rest of the group talked about how much he missed Joan, who became known by the members as the missing blue bird.*

Through this metaphor, which was not easy for either the members or the therapist to understand, Norm was giving voice to his grief. He was attempting to communicate with the therapist and the members indirectly about a matter he could not address directly. Norm was also giving voice to the other members' sadness as well. That is, the metaphor was not only Norm's personal metaphor it was a group metaphor. This is frequently the case in groups. Metaphors that individuals bring into a group are often group metaphors as well. Among the more common topics that become metaphors for the group or therapist are families, places where the members work, priests, police officers, outside doctors, and so on. When group members talk about topics of this nature, therapists can facilitate the interactions and understanding of the group members by drawing attention to the group events to which they point.

Some therapists[12] believe that it is better to allow regressed patients to work out difficulties through metaphors without drawing their attention to the actual difficulties. If group members, for instance, are talking about family conflicts as a metaphor for conflicts among the group members, it is better, they argue, to let the group members work out their differences through that metaphor than to have them talk directly about the group conflict. We believe that a great deal of work can be done through a metaphor, and that the members should be allowed ample opportunity to elaborate on the chosen metaphor. We also believe, however, that with most patients it is also essential that therapists draw the members' attention to the real group issues contained in the metaphor. If therapists permit the members to work issues out only in the metaphor they risk reinforcing the belief that the issue is indeed too dangerous to be talked about directly.

Conferring Meaning.   When interventions are made around metaphors they usually give meaning to a set of experiences and behaviors. When the therapist in our last example drew attention to the relationship between Norm's missing blue bird and Joan's termination he was also giving meaning to Norm's behavior and experience. He was saying, Norm is feeling and behaving the way he is because he is grieving the loss of Joan. Giving meaning to Norm's communication in this manner enabled him to make sense out of his experience and to tolerate it. It also normalized Norm's experience. Although Norm's behavior was indeed strange and unusual, once it was given meaning it became clear that Norm was trying to cope with a very normal human experience: grief over the loss of a friend. He was then able to reconnect with the group members. We have used a metaphor to illustrate the value of conferring meaning. It is important to note, however, that meaning can be given to a wide range of behaviors and not simply to metaphors.

Giving meaning to individual and group experiences is an important function of the group therapist both in inpatient and outpatient settings. The giving of meaning, however, is more limited in inpatient settings. In inpatient groups we believe, for the reasons given earlier, that the meanings given to behavior in groups is better when limited to the relationship of those behaviors to current (here-and-now) events. Therapists can help members contain and master their concerns when they use clarifying interpretations§ to make connections between their behavior and ongoing events, such as the loss of a member, the experience of entering or leaving the hospital, other patients' regressions, therapists' vacations, and so on. That is, when they relate the behaviors to the adaptive context.

In level I groups, so much energy goes into dealing with the beginning process and establishing minimal connections among the members, that conferring meaning may seem to be of little importance. Nevertheless, there are times when giving meaning to behavior in level I groups can also be valuable and necessary. It can make the beginnings smoother and the building of connections easier.

> EXAMPLE. *A level I group was beginning. The members were gradually finding their seats with some assistance from the leaders. One leader brought the members to the group, one and two at a time. The other leader remained in the group room to prevent the members who were present from leaving before the other members arrived. After a great deal of shuffling between chairs the members finally settled down.*
>
> *One of the leaders began to introduce himself to the group. While he was speaking, his colleague rolled up the sleeves of his shirt because the room was very warm. Suddenly, a young woman rose up from her seat and ran into one of the closets. When the leaders asked her to rejoin the group she refused. Her speech was agitated and bizarre and full of sexual references. She stared intently and fearfully at the therapist who had his sleeves rolled up. As he watched her, he realized that she had run into the closet at the moment he rolled up his sleeves and concluded she must have viewed his action as a sexual gesture. So he verbally acknowledged her fear of him and assured her that he would not do her any harm. He said if it would help her he would keep his sleeves rolled down. Shortly after that interchange she rejoined the group and did not leave it again. The other members also settled down and the group got underway.*‖

In this example, giving meaning to the patient's behavior and assuring her that she would be protected enabled her to return to the group. It is not clear if she had any understanding of her own flight before the therapist spoke to her. Maybe she did know and was too frightened to give it words, in which case giving meaning to her behavior would not

---

§ See Chapter 2

‖ This example was first used in a briefer form in: R. W. Betcher, C. A. Rice, and D. M. Wier, "The Regressed Inpatient Group in a Graded Group Treatment Program," *Am. J. Psychother.* 36 (1982):229–239.

have been providing any insight for her. However, it did allow her to know that she was understood. It also enabled the therapist to make helpful comments and gave the members a framework of understanding that enabled them to settle down and come together. In other words, even if giving meaning adds nothing new to a patient's understanding, it builds a network of understanding between the therapist and the patient and between the patient and the other members.

We have suggested some interventions that can be used when leading an inpatient group. We do not offer them as easy techniques that will magically heal patients on the one hand, or provide the therapists wth wonderful dynamic, productive groups on the other. We have no illusions about the difficulty of leading groups with very troubled patients. To lead such groups effectively requires all the knowledge and skill we can muster. Rather, it is our wish that the material in this chapter, creatively integrated by the reader to match the needs of his or her group of patients, will prove helpful.

In the next chapter we discuss some difficult patients and groups that therapists meet in inpatient settings and suggest some approaches to them.

REFERENCES

1. R. Almond, *The Healing Community: Dynamics of the Therapeutic Milieu* (New York: Jason Aronson, 1974).

2. C. A. Rice and J. S. Rutan, "Boundary Maintenance in Inpatient Therapy Groups," *Int. J. Group Psychother*. 31 (1981):305–306.

3. I. R. Rutchick, "Group Psychotherapy" in *Inpatient Psychiatry: Diagnosis and Treatment,* edited by L. I. Sederer (Baltimore: Williams and Wilkins, 1983).

4. J. S. Rutan and W. N. Stone, *Psychodynamic Group Psychotherapy* (New York: Macmillan, 1984), pp. 107–115.

5. M. Day, "The Therapeutic Envelope." Paper presented at meeting of American Group Psychotherapy Association, January 1963.

6. L. E. Hedges, *Listening Perspectives in Psychotherapy* (New York: Jason Aronson, 1983).

7. Hedges, *Listening Perspectives in Psychotherapy*.

8. Hedges, *Listening Perspectives in Psychotherapy*.

9. J. S. Mann, *Time-Limited Psychotherapy*. (Cambridge, Mass: Harvard University Press, 1973).

10. J. S. Maxmen, "An Educative Model for Inpatient Group Therapy," *Int. J. Group Psychother.* 28 (1978):321–337.

11. H. Kellerman, *Group Psychotherapy and Personality: Intersecting Structures* (New York: Grune & Stratton, 1979), pp. 15–37.

12. G. A. Katz, "The Noninterpretation of Metaphors in Psychiatric Hospital Groups," *Int. J. Group Psychother.* 33 (1983):53–67.

7

Difficult Patients and Difficult Groups

There are many occasions when even the most experienced group therapists are unsure about how to respond to a difficult patient or group. We are at times puzzled, overwhelmed, depressed, angry, confused by certain patients and groups, and feel that all our skill and knowledge has little impact. Indeed, it is unlikely that therapists will ever know exactly how to respond to all the difficult patients and groups they will face. Because inpatient group therapists are confronted with groups of individuals in particular crisis and upheaval, it is inevitable that they will be confronted with difficult patients and groups.

There are some general approaches that can be taken toward these patients and groups that can be useful, particularly if therapists avoid the trap of turning those approaches into rigid rules. Hearing and understanding patients must always take precedence over the blind application of guidelines, no matter how helpful they may seem.

When faced with difficult patients or groups, therapists should be alert to the fact that countertransference may be contributing to the difficulty. As we noted in Chapter 6, countertransference responses are often a serious barrier to the effective leadership of groups and can be the source of considerable discomfort between patients and therapists. If countertransference is contributing to the difficulty with a patient or a group it needs to be acknowledged and understood by the therapists. Often when that is done the patient or the group is no longer so difficult.

DIFFICULT PATIENTS

A variety of patients can be difficult for group therapists. Sometimes the difficulty therapists experience with a group member is related to diagnosis. A manic–depressive patient, for instance, may cause considerable difficulty for therapists during manic and hypomanic episodes. At other times, specific patient behaviors, such as excessive anger, may create difficulties for the therapist. Other patients may be difficult to work with because they are the spokespersons for some or all of the group members and for some or all of the hospital community as well as for themselves, thus making individual interventions much less effective. Then again, a few patients or types of patients may be difficult for one therapist and not for another. At times this is due to therapist countertransference.

In this section, we suggest interventions for dealing with difficult patients where the difficulty may be due in whole or in part to each of these situations.

PARTICULAR EMOTIONAL DISORDERS

In this section we examine (1) the thought-disordered patient, (2) the manic–depressive patient, (3) the borderline patient, and (4) the narcissistic patient.

Thought-Disordered Patients.   One traditional way of distinguishing between diagnoses is to differentiate between individuals who are thought disordered, affectively disordered, and character disordered. Thought-disordered patients exhibit thought patterns that are not easily followed by others, and they are typically diagnosed as being psychotic. Because they use different patterns of logic and thought than most, they can be very hard to understand and not infrequently stimulate anxiety in therapists. Their participation in the group is difficult to comprehend because they follow their own internal rules, and they sometimes appear isolated and distracted or talk about matters that seem to bear no relevance to the group discussion, using neologisms and idiosyncratic metaphors that disrupt the flow of the session.

One must remember that the term *thought disordered* is a value judgment, and that from the patients' perspective their thoughts are completely "ordered." The therapeutic task, from a psychodynamic perspective, is to break the code, to find out the fundamental assumptions from which these patients begin, and in light of which all their thoughts are coherent. Despite how difficult it may be to understand the thought-disordered patient, the therapist should assume that the patients' behavior is an attempt to communicate and that the communication, more often than not, is about the patients' overall treatment including group therapy.[1,2] These patients' unusual behaviors are often an attempt to cope with overwhelming fears of annihilation and of dissolution of the self.

There are at least two strategies that are helpful when confronted with thought disorders in a particular group meeting. Sometimes therapists can help patients cope with their fear by clarifying the patients' metaphors and generalizing them to the whole group, as we illustrated with the patient who lost his blue bird.* This has the benefits of making the "strange thoughts" less frightening to both the patient and the other group members, which in turn facilitates future investigation of free associative material, as well as building empathic understanding of the thought-disordered patient from the others. At another time it may be helpful to guide the patient firmly, but gently, back into the flow of the group. This approach has the advantage of reminding thought-disordered patients that their behavior, although perhaps eventually understandable by highly compassionate and tolerant individuals, is nonetheless unusual and not typically acceptable in society. It helps these patients begin to distinguish between primary and secondary thinking.

> EXAMPLE. *A level II group was being used for teaching purposes, and thus was being observed by most of the hospital staff. Due to this irregularity, attendance at the group was on a voluntary basis for the patients, and two chose not to participate. Much of the conversation in the group centered on what it was like to be observed, the anxiety about attending, and the courage it took to be present.*
>
> *During the session one of the members, Rob, remained particularly quiet, staring at the ceiling for much of the time. Late in the meeting he began to talk. He was very confused and made little sense to others. He said he had been talking to his dead uncle, a beloved man and one of the major supports in his life.*
>
> *Clearly, Rob was frightened and confused and needed his uncle now. Under the stress of the observed group, he had temporarily exhibited the behavior he displayed in the level I group from which he had recently graduated.*

---

* See Chapter 6, pp. 126–127.

In this example the therapist could have taken either approach. Had he determined to opt for the former approach, the patient's verbalizations would have been interpreted as his wish to have his beloved uncle to protect and soothe him in this anxious situation. The goal of this intervention would be to help the patient understand that his thoughts were not random, and to help the other group members understand their colleague better and, therefore, to have the opportunity to investigate how each of them was coping with their anxieties in the current situation.

In fact, in this case the therapist determined that the presence of observers made the patients feel too vulnerable for an interpretation, and thus addressed Rob's anxiety and confusion by cognitively clarifying what was going on. He told Rob where he was and what he was doing. He described the group and reintroduced the members to him, pointed out the staff who were observing and thanked him for having the courage to participate in the group. Rob agreed that it took courage to be present, relaxed, and was much more comprehendible during the remainder of the group.

Manic–Depressive Patients.   Manic–depressive patients often enter the hospital during acute manic episodes. During those episodes it is unlikely that they will be able to benefit from any group, even a level I group. After the initial crisis has passed and medication has removed the more excessive aspects of the manic episode they can usually begin group treatment. However, they are often quite dominating in groups, talking nonstop, and having little concern about the other members. Beginning therapists can be easily intimidated, frightened, and enraged by them. It is helpful to remember, however, that these patients are often as frightened as they are frightening, and that having someone place a limit on their excessive talking can be a great relief for them. That limit should be set as a way of reducing their anxiety and not as a means of punishing bad or unwanted behavior. A limit can be set most effectively if the therapist first allies with these patients and helps them maintain their sense of importance.[3] It is helpful to acknowledge the issues the patients have raised and suggest firmly that the patients and therapist together see what other members of the group have to say about those issues. Sometimes, after a very brief contribution by another patient, the manic patient will talk again. It is helpful if the therapist intervenes quickly and says words such as "I think we should give the members more time to respond."

Once in a great while a manic patient will give the therapist a metaphor that can be used to set limits and support the patient.

EXAMPLE. *Sally talked excessively and dominated the group. She spoke at length about her driving. She told how she drove in a fast and reckless manner and had difficulty stopping even at traffic lights. The therapist noted that she seemed to be having difficulty negotiating the traffic in the group and that it might help if he acted as a traffic signal for her. She said it would. They agreed that if she talked too much and too fast the therapist should give a red light signal by raising his hand, then she would stop. This procedure worked and helped contain her anxiety until she was able to contain it for herself a few sessions later.*

This is another example of how inpatient therapists must be somewhat more active than outpatient therapists. In an outpatient group the therapist would allow one member to dominate a group for much longer in hopes that the other members would eventually confront the behavior. The short-term and transitory nature of an inpatient group mandates that the therapist assume a more active leadership role, though the goal is still to help the other members gain some capacity also to confront the behaviors of individuals.

Borderline Patients. Borderline patients' capacity for instant and intense emotional attachments, sudden withdrawals, outbursts of rage, destructive behaviors, and varied symptomatology can make them problematic members of any group. Because they will generate a great deal of affect and interaction among the group members, both pleasant and unpleasant, they can also be very valuable members of a group. Groups of which they are members are rarely dull.

Borderline patients are experts at getting attention. Therapists can readily get caught in the dilemma of being too involved with or too removed from borderline patients.[4] Seduction through sexuality, helplessness, idealization of the therapists, and an apparent willingness to be good patients can readily cause therapists to take an overly sympathetic attitude toward them. By contrast, the tendency of these patients, on other occasions, to attack and denigrate therapists and groups can readily cause therapists to remain distant from them. The dilemma can take other forms. Therapists can sometimes develop a masochistic relationship with these patients as they allow their unremitting rage to beat on them, whereas at other times, they may take a punitive and sadistic stance. As we noted in Chapter 2, the therapists' dilemma is generated by these patients' yearnings to merge on the one hand, and their fear of it on the other, and by their need to view themselves and others in terms of "good" and "bad" objects. This method of organizing their internal and interpersonal worlds means that they are sometimes the recipients and, at other times, the progenitors of sadistic behavior.

It is important that therapists maintain clear boundaries with these patients while allowing them to be as close or as distant as they need to be. An optimal distance can be maintained if therapists make group-wide interventions around the issues these patients raise and avoid being seduced into intimate and individual investigation of their concerns. The example of Maude's relationship to her therapist† illustrates this point.

> EXAMPLE. *Immediately following her first group session, Maude pleaded with the therapist to transfer her to another group. The therapist found himself strongly drawn to Maude, even though he hardly knew her, which made it more difficult than usual for him to address her request. However, he managed to maintain his composure well enough to ask her to bring up her request during the next session. Before the next session he learned that the head nurse felt equally strongly about Maude, but was repelled by her rather than drawn to her. This information helped the therapist to put his own feelings in perspective.*
>
> *During the next session Maude raised the issue of the transfer and rallied members of the group behind her. She was very angry. The therapist stated that some sessions can be more difficult than others, and that one can readily feel like leaving. He suggested that it might be well for Maude to talk about the feelings she had about joining the group, and he indicated his conviction that talking about the feelings would do her more good than transferring to a different group. Initially, Maude's anger increased, and then she settled down.*

Borderline patients are experts at manipulating people. It is one of their primary survival mechanisms, and we should not begrudge their willingness to use it. Maude had probably sensed the merger taking place between herself and the therapist and tried to use it to her advantage. She was also probably trying to find a way to establish a comfortable distance from the therapist. His nonsadistic firmness in maintaining the group contract helped to provide the appropriate distance.

Narcissistic Patients.   In contrast with borderline patients, narcissistic patients may seem free of personal concerns. Others may have

---

† See Chapter 6, pp. 113–114, for a more complete illustration of this example.

problems, but not them. They may be looked up to and admired by some of the group members who may prefer their leadership to that of the therapists'. They do not relate easily with those who do not need them or wish to follow and admire them and may cut them down with a few well-chosen words if they challenge anything they say.

Also in contrast with borderline patients, narcissistic patients are not well attuned to others. Indeed, they seem unconcerned with the needs of other people, viewing them solely as supplies for their own personal needs. Typically, narcissistic patients do not engender the passionate responses that borderline patients do. One diagnostic sign that a patient is highly narcissistic is that they are often boring to sit with. This is because they seem to give so little back in a relationship, as their primary concern is with getting from others what they need to survive.

At the same time, they are hypersensitive to criticism. Therapists often feel incompetent and irrelevant when working with them and their comments seem to have little impact.[5] When narcissistic patients do greatly admire their therapists, that admiration may dissipate quickly and be given to others considered more admirable. Likewise, with the same fickleness, they may consider the group and the hospital alternately the greatest group and hospital ever, or the worst.

Narcissistic patients develop what Kohut[6-8] describes as selfobject relationships. Other people are seen as extensions of themselves, some as admirers who mirror their grandiose sense of themselves, whereas others become projections of their grandiose selves who they will then admire. People who are unwilling to be part of that selfobject relationship are quickly dismissed.

These patients may appear so suave and in charge, or so unmoved by events that readily move others, that therapists will often urge them to say what they are feeling and push them toward greater introspection. As the patients continue unmoved therapists may press harder and become increasingly unempathic toward them. The increasing loss of empathy is due to the therapists' failure to recognize that to maintain a viable sense of self these patients need to reduce the impact that others have on them, including therapists. If one has an impact on another he or she is no longer a selfobject.

To be effective therapists should do as little as possible and tolerate the feeling of not being a very good therapist or of being greatly admired without being fooled by either. In time, as trust builds within the group and toward the therapists, these patients will be able to allow sufficient closeness to permit them to function adequately in the group. It is important that therapists not expect great changes in these patients during their stay in the group but rather see their work as preparatory to the essential long-term therapy that will follow discharge. Perhaps most important of all, it is imperative that therapists remember that these individuals, like all others, are doing the best they can to gain and sustain relationships with others. Due to the noxious side effects that often accompany their particular strategies, therapists are often persuaded that these individuals do not really *want* or *need* a relationship, which ironically is the final defense used by these patients. They, too, often try to believe they do not really need any others in their lives.

SPECIFIC DIFFICULT BEHAVIORS

There are some problematic behaviors that occur with sufficient regularity to warrant special attention. These behaviors can occur across diagnostic categories. Patients from a wide variety of diagnoses, for instance, can become group dominators. Manic–depressive patients can dominate a group during a hypomanic phase, alcoholic patients can dominate with stories about their drinking, anxious patients can talk anxiously, and so forth.

In this section we discuss four types of problematic behavior that occur regularly in therapy groups: (1) patients who interrupt the group process, (2) patients who are sadistic and hurtful, (3) patients who dominate, and (4) patients who are highly anxious. It is important to note that in these instances we are talking about extreme behavior. We do not suggest that every time a patient seems angry or upset that therapists need to make special interventions to keep them in line or to ease their discomfort. We are now referring to behaviors that may seriously threaten the safety and usefulness of the group or threaten the capacity of the difficult patients to benefit from the group. These are usually behaviors that cannot be addressed effectively by the difficult patients themselves or by the group members, especially in a time-limited inpatient group.

Patients Who Interrupt the Group Process. Patients who intrude into group conversations with comments that kill the mood of the group, break up the flow of the conversation, and make it nearly impossible for the other members to continue are a source of concern to therapists. Interruptions of this nature are particularly common in level I groups. Often the intruding patients are very self-absorbed, do not consciously hear what is being said, and therefore introduce material that seems to be unconnected with what has been going on before. Clearly, it is better if the group members themselves can limit the intrusive member's behavior, but often this is not possible, particularly in a group of severely regressed patients. Under these circumstances, it is important that therapists intervene directly.

It must be remembered that the intruding patient is not really being boorish on purpose, but rather that this patient is protecting him or herself in the best way he or she knows. Therapists must counter the wish to punish. One can usually begin by thanking the intruding patients for their ✓ contributions and their willingness to participate, and reassuring them that they will have an opportunity later to talk about the matters they have raised. In the meantime they must let the other members finish what they were saying. It is important, as well, to indicate to the member (and, therefore, at the same time to the group) that the therapist understands that this behavior is serving some function that will ultimately be understood. The other members should then be encouraged to continue their interactions.

> EXAMPLE. *The members of a level I group were slowly and tentatively getting to know each other. With help from the therapists they were telling each other their names interspersed with claims from Ted that he was the Messiah. As Toni was gingerly giving her name, Ted interrupted again saying with emphasis "I* am *the Messiah" and proceeded to talk about how much he knew and could do. Toni was frightened as were the other members. One of the therapists turned to Ted and said, "You* are *a very important person, you're very important in this group." "Yes I am" said Ted, "everybody is." The therapist agreed with Ted and told him that Toni should continue telling her name and then later the therapist would return to Ted. Shortly after Toni and a few others had given their names, the therapists and the group returned to Ted and talked about being important. Not much was said by the members, but Ted was able to emphasize again that he was the Messiah and very important and so was everyone in the group.*

Patients who interrupt should be addressed respectfully as well as firmly. Although most interruptions may seem tangential and irrelevant, they are usually important to the person making the interruption and, not uncommonly, as with Ted, contain a communication to the members. Ted helped this group bond, albeit in a very primitive manner, by emphasizing everyone's importance.

Patients Who Are Sadistic and Hurtful.   Patients who are openly sadistic and verbally assault the therapists and the members can readily threaten the safety of any group and quickly undermine the therapists' effectiveness. We are now referring to individuals who actively seek to inflict pain. This behavior is to be distinguished from the sharing of negative feelings, which of course is to be encouraged. Ormont[9] makes such a distinction in his contract with members, allowing the expression of feeling but not attacking other members. Members are likely to become increasingly anxious if therapists mildly accept such hurtful assaults or permit them to be inflicted on other group members. They will fear that they too may be assaulted or lose control of their anger and begin assaulting others.

These patients are often at their most assaultive during their first session when they are most anxious about being in the group. By assaulting and frightening others, they are trying to defend themselves against that anxiety. Their philosophy seems to be, "A good offense is the best defense." Therapists should intervene as early as possible to reduce their anxiety and so prevent the assaults from escalating unnecessarily. They should welcome these patients to the group and link their noxious behavior to their joining the group. The therapist must also begin at once distinguishing between speaking one's feelings and using sadism to drive others away. Often this is sufficient to reduce the new patient's anxiety and that of the rest of the group so that all may continue with their work. In instances where these patients do not respond to therapists' interventions it may be necessary to remove them from the group with the understanding that they can return when they have given indication that they are able to participate without harming others.

If patients are asked to leave it is important that therapists encourage the remaining members to talk about that event. Removing patients from groups is a rare and powerful event, and it has a profound effect on those who remain. If it is done judiciously it will likely provide relief and safety for the others, but it will raise other concerns as well. Members will wonder who will be next to leave? How can I express my anger? If I express my feelings will I be thrown out? These and many other concerns result from such an important act.

On the other hand, if the patients were asked to leave for reasons that had more to do with therapists' countertransference responses than patients' needs, then the ensuing conversations of the members take on even greater importance. Those conversations inform therapists about their errors and give them and the members an opportunity to address the increased danger in the group and begin to reestablish safety.

Sometimes, therapists' own fears and concerns can prevent them from setting limits soon enough.

EXAMPLE. *Tom was a large, gregarious, adolescent male. He entered his first group by shouting loudly and swearing liberally. He threw himself into a chair that barely withstood his impact and began cursing and behaving in a threatening and belligerent manner. The therapist was taken aback, as were the rest of the group. One man in the group asked Tom to settle down, he'd had enough of his antics on the unit, and didn't want to see them in his group as well. A shouting match ensued that threatened to become a fist fight. The therapist intervened and made clear to both parties that they were perfectly welcome to say what was on their mind but fights of this nature would not be tolerated. Tom swore at the therapist, but then settled down. Tom was then introduced to the members and the group proceeded somewhat uneasily. They talked tentatively about how frightened they had felt of Tom and of his behavior on the unit and wondered if he should be in this group. Tom seemed to mellow. He made an occasional angry comment but otherwise remained within the bounds of the group.*

However, Tom's difficulties with the group did not abate as easily as the therapist and the members had hoped. During the next several sessions he again attacked the therapist and the members. Finally, the therapist asked him to leave the group, only to have Tom return in the next session to cause havoc again. The therapist was puzzled by her own ineffectiveness and her slowness to set limits on Tom. Although she had asked him to leave the group she realized that she had been unduly slow to do so. In addition, she had not made any clear stipulation about what behavior was expected from Tom before he could return to the group. The therapist had also learned from colleagues that Tom was not just a problem for her but for all the staff. He was creating chaos throughout the unit and seemed incorrigible. After further conversations with the staff and some self-examination the therapist realized that several factors were getting in the way of effectively responding to this angry and troubled young man. Despite his behavior the therapist found Tom likeable and was nursing the secret fantasy that by doing good "therapy" she could help him—even though all the staff put together had been unable to do so. She also feared that if she refused to let Tom attend the group Tom would be delighted and other patients would follow his lead and also leave. Having dealt with those narcissistic fantasies the therapist, with the help of the staff, set much firmer limits on Tom. Tom was told in advance that if he began swearing and shouting at the therapist or members of the group he would have to leave. He would be placed in the locked unit, and could not return until he was able to control his behavior. Tom was quiet for a while, but

*soon told the therapist in no uncertain terms just what she could do with
her group! He was immediately placed in the locked unit. For the next
three days, much to the therapist's surprise, Tom talked constantly about
wanting to get back into the group. When he did return he was able to
contain himself and work well in the group.*

The therapist had underestimated the anger and fear that Tom experienced and his limited capacity to contain it. She also underestimated how much Tom wanted contact with others. She had believed that if she asked him to leave for a period of time he'd be only too glad to do so. Tom was caught in the conflict between his desire to have relationships with his peers, and his fear of them and of his own impulses. The therapist's countertransference reactions had blinded her to those fears and yearnings and prevented her from setting appropriate limits.

Patients Who Dominate.   Most difficult patients dominate groups. But there are some who can dominate groups without being particularly difficult in other ways. They may dominate the group through their eagerness, enthusiasm, inability to allow others to join in the conversation, or by constantly telling others what to do, and so on. These patients can often be helpful in getting groups going and in helping quieter group members participate. Over time, however, this behavior becomes more difficult to tolerate and more problematic for the group.

As discussed before, therapists should always acknowledge the participation of patients in their most positive light, even when going on to set limits. In this case, therapists can note the effort the patients have been making to be involved in the group, and to recognize that they have served a valuable function in getting discussions underway. Therapists should also recognize that group domination is not a one-party game, and that the entire group has played a role in the domination by one individual. To that end, the therapist can suggest that others carry some of that responsibility as well. It can also be helpful to select one of the many issues raised by these patients and ask that other members share their thoughts about it. When dominating patients try to move on to other issues therapists should let them know that not everyone has responded and that each member should be given a reasonable opportunity to participate. Again acknowledging the positive sides, it might be useful for the therapist to add a comment such as, "Perhaps the group does not need your assistance at this moment."

EXAMPLE. *Paul and Robin joined a group at the same time, and it seemed clear that they would be valuable additions to the group. They talked easily and others responded to them. They had both entered the hospital because of alcohol problems. They told the group how alcohol had ruined their lives and inflicted pain on their families. They swapped numerous stories with each other. Others joined in. The therapists found the group very easy to lead. This, they thought, was a truly interactive meeting.*

The next day the group began in a similar manner. Paul and Robin swapped more stories. Some members began talking about concerns not related to alcohol and Paul and Robin were again happy to help. They jumped in with numerous suggestions about how the patients could help themselves. The suggestions were strategies they had learned from A.A., which they illustrated liberally from their own experience. Invariably the discussion reverted back to alcohol and themselves. As the meeting progressed, fewer and fewer members participated. The therapists made several leading comments to encourage others to participate, but with little success. Any responses came primarily from Paul or Robin. The group was no longer the wonderful interactive group they had observed in the preceding session. Finally, one of the therapists turned to Paul and Robin and acknowledged verbally how much effort they had been making to keep things going in the group. They readily agreed and talked about how they also did it at A.A. and liked doing it. More firmly the therapist said, "I think, like at A.A., we can best help the group if the others can be en- ✓ couraged to tell their stories and carry some of the load." Very slowly others began to respond. They had been tired of talking about alcohol. For a time the group was very tense and Paul and Robin were initially hurt by the other members' responses. But as the members acknowledged how helpful they had been at the beginning, Paul and Robin slowly accepted the fact that it probably was fair to talk about other things besides alcohol.

It was very important to acknowledge that Paul and Robin had been truly helpful to the group during its dependency phase. They had provided a common theme around which the members could bond. Their own difficulty in differentiating, however, made it hard for them to give up that role and recognize the members' desires to move beyond that point. No doubt the members' own uncertainty about differentiating made it difficult for them to challenge their role.

Patients Who Are Highly Anxious.   Some patients feel so anxious that they cannot tolerate being in a group. In those cases it is usually best to openly recognize their difficulties and praise them for being able to stay as long as they did. They should then be permitted to leave with the understanding that they are *not* only expected, but are welcome to return to the next session, at which time they may be able to stay longer. A very anxious patient may take several visits before being able to stay for a whole meeting. Other patients, whose anxiety is less overwhelming may be able to sit outside the group circle and observe until they feel safe enough to enter, whereas others may be relieved by being able to pace outside the group for a time. Having an area in which to pace can be particularly helpful for patients experiencing psychomotor agitation √ in response to medication.

It is important that therapists be particularly sensitive to these patients' discomfort and not push them beyond what they can bear, and at the same time respect that part of them that wishes to remain in or make contact with the other members. At times it is difficult to distinguish between the error of colluding with a patient's pathology and respecting his defenses.

> EXAMPLE. *A level I group was about to begin. The therapists were bringing the members to the group one and two at a time. One of the therapists met a new group member, Phyllis, in the hallway and reminded her that it was time to go to group. The prospect of entering the group truly frightened her. She did not speak; she merely shook her head and looked quite terrified. The therapist, recognizing her fear said, "You seem frightened about the group. Perhaps you would rather wait and join tomorrow." He continued to bring other patients to the group. As he did, Phyllis followed him down the hall to the door of the group room but did not go in. Sensing Phyllis's mixture of anxiety and curiosity about the other members, he said "Would you like to sit in the hallway by the door and watch the group?" She nodded her head. So she was given a chair outside the group room door from which she watched the group. The leaders told the other members that Phyllis was feeling too frightened to come into the group right now but would watch from the door. No one objected.*
>
> *Phyllis watched from the door for two sessions. On the third session she sat inside the room by the door and watched, and on the fourth session she entered the group. After that she became an active and ardent member until she graduated to a level II group.*

SHARED GROUP OR COMMUNITY-WIDE CONCERNS

Given the isomorphic nature of the relationships in a group and on a unit, one can assume that difficult patients always give voice to issues that are concerns for others as well. But there are occasions when the collusion between the difficult patient's behavior and the concerns of other patients is much more central.

Clues as to when there is a group collusion surrounding a difficult patient are usually found in the behavior of the group members and in the derivative material. When the collusion becomes clear it is the therapist's task to enable the other members to become aware of and talk about their collusion and voice their concerns directly. When this is done the difficult patient usually becomes much less difficult.

EXAMPLE. *Steve, an adolescent, entered a group that was made up largely of adults, a few minutes after it had begun. He said he wanted to be excused from this session because his mother was visiting the hospital. His mother often visited the hospital and would be around for most of the day. The therapist reminded him of his agreement to attend and to stay for the whole session. He insisted, however, that he should go. He then turned to the other members and asked them what they thought. Most of the group members were quite depressed, so the responses came slowly. As he went round the room all the members felt that he should indeed go. But he did not leave. Rather, he turned again to the therapist and asked what he thought. The therapist said he thought Steve should stay. Steve turned to the group again and said, "O.K. if one other person says I shouldn't leave, I'll stay. But I think I should go. What do you think?" Again, all agreed he should be able to go. He left.*

The session continued to move very slowly. What conversation there was focused on Steve and his mother. Members spoke of how nice it was for Steve to want to see his mother rather than be at the group. The therapist suggested that there may be others who'd rather be somewhere else than in the group. No, they thought the group was a nice group. The group continued on its slow and measured pace. Later the group therapist pressed again. This time one person said she'd rather be elsewhere. She noted that it was a nice day out and this group wasn't going very well. The session came to an end.

At the beginning of the next session Steve was missing. The members were again very quiet and withdrawn. The therapist noted Steve's absence. One member said he's with his mother as he should be. Again the matter of his being a nice boy with his mother came up, and once again the therapist raised the possibility that others may prefer to be elsewhere, too. This time the response was stronger. Several members felt the group was too slow and that the therapist wasn't doing very much to help. Gradually most members spoke of how dissatisfied they were with the group. One particularly perceptive member admitted that he was cheering Steve's decision to leave. He wished he had had as good an excuse. During these exchanges Steve arrived and sat listening. Then he spoke. "Hey, its good to hear some talking going on in here. This group was so damned dull. Nobody gave a shit about anybody. I said I'd stay if just one of you said I shouldn't leave. But nobody did, so I left."

Steve had spoken and acted out the anger of the whole group. If the therapist had focused on Steve to the exclusion of the other members, his acting out probably would have continued unabated and resulted in increasing struggles with the staff. The anger of the other members would also have continued unspoken and unresolved.

SUMMARY

In dealing with the difficult patient, therapists have essentially three strategies for responding. The first is to interpret the "troublesome" behavior to help the patient and the group understand the protective qualities that the behavior provides. These patients are demonstrating one of their primary defenses against the terrors that life holds for them, and if it is possible to interpret the behaviors without endangering the effectiveness of the group, this is obviously the best choice of intervention.

Second, the therapist can help the individual and the group understand that the offensive behavior is actually serving a group-wide or community-wide function. This function can be the communicating of some unspeakable truth (such as, "None of us like this group or this leader!") or the titrating of anxiety by diverting the group's attention to the offending member. When a group is using a specific individual for these purposes it is often most evident by how the group prompts the patient to begin talking or behaving in troublesome ways when the patient has temporarily ceased them.

Finally, if the therapist deems it inadvisable to use interpretation, because the patient or the group, or both, cannot tolerate the situation long enough for that to take effect, then the therapist must set some limits. Hopefully this limit setting can occur in a manner in which the patient in question is not severely wounded. There will always be some narcissistic wounding when such behavior is limited because the limitation inevitably implies that the behavior is "bad."

Difficult Groups

Difficult patients usually create difficult groups. But there are many occasions when a group can be difficult even though there are no especially difficult patients among the members. From this perspective some might argue that all inpatient groups are difficult to lead. There are times, however, when the difficulties are much more demanding than at others.

In this section we discuss some examples of groups that can be particularly difficult. They are the depressed, passive, angry, and chaotic groups.

THE DEPRESSED GROUP

Depressed groups are difficult to lead because the depression of the members may seem overwhelming. Therapists' interventions and comments seem to have little impact, and, not surprisingly, the therapists may end up feeling inadequate and quite depressed themselves.

The depressed mood of these groups may be due to the fact that most of the members are suffering from depression and are feeling particularly demoralized at this time, or they may be feeling sad and depressed in response to a recent hospital or group event. Those events may include such things as therapists' vacations, the deterioration of a group member, special holidays, the termination of a fellow patient, and so on. When especially serious events affect the ward, such as the suicide of a patient or an incident of physical violence, these inevitably affect the groups as well.

As with most difficult groups the initial task of the therapist is to tolerate the affect of the group and listen to whatever clues the members may give about their concerns. If the therapist knows that a particular recent incident in the hospital may be contributing to the members' depression, it is important that he or she introduce the matter fairly early so that there is adequate time to talk about it. If the therapist is correct in linking some recent incident to the present group's depression, it is very likely that the members will begin to participate more actively. If the group continues to be unresponsive after the therapist has addressed what appears to be the members' concerns, it can be helpful to go around the group talking to the members one by one about whatever topic may have been introduced. Sometimes that topic may be nothing more than the fact that it seems to be very hard to talk in the group. Those round the room interventions should also include attempts by the therapist to make connections among the members, by noting the commonality of their concerns and encouraging members to talk more to each other about those concerns. If the round the room intervention is done with sensitivity to the patients' limited capacities to respond, the therapist may learn something of what their concerns are, but, more importantly he or she will have begun to establish or reestablish interactions and alliances with and among the members. As Betcher[10] has noted, the group cohesion that emerges out of these interactions is effective in countering the demoralization inpatients often experience.

In these groups the dilemma for therapists is being able to live within the limits set by the depression. The sense of powerlessness generated by the depression sometimes triggers angry responses or disinterest in therapists as well as sadness. Unfortunately, when one is angry it is only too easy to use round the room and other interventions to subtly interrogate the members in the hope of provoking them into responses. By contrast, disinterest can lead therapists to disengage altogether from the patients and leave them to drift in their depression. It is important that therapists remain engaged with the patient and be willing to address their sense of despair and inability to "get going" without interrogating them as a protection against their own despair.

> EXAMPLE. *The group was smaller than usual. There were three patients, Pat, Ron and Sam and two female therapists. Five of the members had not yet returned after the weekend. No one spoke.*
>
> *One of the therapists asked Pat how his weekend had been. "O.K. I guess." He then added that he was being discharged soon and was feeling scared. There was a long silence, then Ron said, "The group's getting smaller." A long depressed silence followed. The second therapist asked Ron to say more about the group being small. After another long pause Ron looked at the clock and noted that there were only five minutes left. Then he realized that the clock must have been stopped by a power-outage caused by the hurricane on Friday and corrected himself. With some encouragement from the therapists Pat spoke again. He felt the only way out for him was to kill himself. He then laughed at his voices who had told him to "go forth into the wilderness" during the hurricane. Through gentle and steady engagement by the therapists the members gradually outlined their sadness and despair. Pat told how he would miss the "guys" if he was discharged. Like so many things in his life he seemed to have little control over when he was leaving. Ron, who was 50, spoke of how hard life was for "old people." "My father died when he was 55," he said. "My brother died a year and a half ago." said Sam. "This brings back all those feelings. I can't talk anymore." They all noted that the Thanksgiving and Christmas holidays were going to be a hard time. Pat went over to the water cooler, drank a glass of cold water and returned to his seat. The group came to an end.*

Through the persistent but gentle urging of the therapists, the members of this group were able to move beneath their depression to the concerns that produced it. As they spoke of their feelings for one another, and their grief at losing the relationships, their depression was replaced by a more manageable and authentic sadness.

THE PASSIVE GROUP

Depressed groups are usually passive groups in that the level of activity is very low. But the groups we are concerned with in this section are those where the passivity is primarily generated in response to covert anger rather than depression and where the membership is comprised of patients who cope through passive resistance. The passive resistance is often in response to feelings about events on the unit or in the group that the members perceive as threatening or enraging. These events can include such things as a drug search (or a failure to do one), a member being placed in seclusion, the leader being late, an earlier intervention by the leader that may have injured a member and created anxiety for others, the addition of an unexpected or unwanted member, observer, or co-leader, and so on. In addition, the primary affect generated in therapists by these groups is more likely to be anger rather than sadness.

In leading these groups it is important that therapists be aware that the members are often very afraid of angry feelings and have a great deal of difficulty asserting themselves directly. Hence, what little response therapists get from the members either individually or collectively should be acknowledged and encouraged. In addition their passive resistance should be recognized as one important way of coping and making their concerns known. After all, a great deal of social change has been brought about by passive resistance. Acknowledging the validity of their resistance also frees the members to consider other possibilities, most specifically that of talking about the events that have generated their anger.

The danger for therapists in leading these groups is to act out their frustrations and those of the members in ways that may seem quite reasonable. For instance, some inexperienced therapists have been known to end sessions early with groups of this nature. "After all," they say, the members had said all they were going to say and nothing else seemed to be going on, so we decided to finish early." The decision, although done with good intentions, is often a retaliation against the members' passivity. It also risks confirming the members' perception of anger as dangerous by seeming to drive the leaders away.

> EXAMPLE. *A young therapist was puzzled by his group and asked his supervisor for help. His group had two observers and nine members, several of whom joined in this session. The observers were therapists in training. At the beginning of the session in question the therapist introduced the new members. No sooner were the new members introduced than Susan raised a vehement objection to having observers in the group. The therapist was surprised by her forcefulness. There had always been observers in the groups, and the patients knew about them before they joined. She complained that medical students were O.K. but not these students. The therapist asked the observers to leave and described the remainder of the session to his supervisor as a "paranoid, stony silence." No one spoke and attempts on his part to engage the members were completely unsuccessful. He was also puzzled by his own willingness to ask the observers to leave.*
>
> *As he discussed the group with his supervisor, he recalled some of the opening remarks in the group that he had previously forgotten. When he arrived at the group the members were involved in a debate about the "three-minute rule." The three-minute rule, instituted sometime earlier by the hospital, said that patients who were more than three minutes late for a group session could not attend that session. They talked about how Robert had been excluded from his last session by that rule. Robert was a young patient who had killed himself about three weeks earlier. His suicide had never been openly talked about by the hospital community.*
>
> *The next session began silently with some murmuring about the previous session. The therapist acknowledged the murmuring and noted how difficult that session had been for all. He further noted that he felt people were still feeling very upset and angry about Robert's death. He wondered if his having excluded the observers last week might not have renewed their memories of Robert, who committed suicide shortly after having been excluded from the group. The group changed dramatically, the members became openly angry about Robert's death, about his being excluded from his group, and about the staff's failure to protect them and him. They spoke about their own feelings of guilt as well.*

The observers had become the focus of some of the members' unresolved anger and grief about Robert's death. However, when the therapist asked the observers to leave so readily he not only removed a displacement target for their anger, but he also confirmed their fantasies about the power and destructiveness of their rage. Consequently, the members regressed into a passive, angry position that they were unable to leave until the legitimacy of their concerns was acknowledged.

THE ANGRY GROUP

The angry group is often the counterpoint of the depressed or passive group. The angry group often has members who cope with life's frustrations by outbursts of anger and rage. Thus, when incidents take place on the unit or in the group similar to those described for the first two groups, they respond with anger rather than depression or passivity. Therapists may have difficulty with these groups because the intensity and tenacity of their anger may be difficult to bear, understand, and limit.

As with other groups most is gained if the therapist can help the members name the concerns and frustrations that are avoided and find expression in the anger.

> EXAMPLE. *The atmosphere was very tense. The members complained loudly and forcefully about how their records were being used and abused. Anybody could look at their records they claimed, and they believed strongly that that was wrong.*
>
> *The therapist was experienced in running inpatient groups, and she did not wilt under the heat of the group's anger. Rather, she listened for the content of the rage and eventually said, "There is a great deal of anger about the public nature of one's records. I wonder if you are finding it hard to reveal yourselves in front of others here in the group?" The initial reaction, of course, was more rage and abuse as the members discounted the leader's comment. Soon, however, the tone of the meeting changed and the members began talking to each other rather than yelling.*

THE CHAOTIC GROUP

These groups can be the most frightening of all the groups for therapists to face. Chaotic groups usually reflect a breakdown of individual and group cohesion in response to events that the members find overwhelming. Usually a lot of seemingly unrelated activity is going on at the same time, such as some members failing to show up, others arriving late, some storming out of the room, others lying on the floor rather than sitting on chairs, numbers of patients talking at once in a disorganized and frightening manner, and so on. Sometimes groups that begin as angry groups can deteriorate into chaotic groups if reasonable limits are not set on the members' rage. Groups of severely and acutely regressed patients, such as level I groups, can readily become chaotic if the therapists are overly passive.

Chaotic groups require direct and firm intervention by the therapists. Initially this might include such basics as asking everyone to sit down and talk one at a time. If possible the therapists should name clearly and firmly the incident that has generated chaos and encourage the members to talk about it.

> EXAMPLE.‡ *A therapist arrived at his first group of the day to find it in shambles. Some patients were lying on the floor, another weeping uncontrollably, another hyperventilating, and so on. The therapist learned from his co-therapist, who had arrived before him, that a young police officer had tried to stop a patient from running away by firing shots into the air. The patients had responded with panic.*
>
> *The therapists quickly called the group to order and began talking about the incident, acknowledging that it was indeed frightening, but that no one was going to come to any harm. It was not until the following session that the group was able to settle down completely. But by the end of that session they were considerably more contained than at the beginning.*

In summary, it is sometimes necessary, when addressing the needs of difficult groups or patients to *lead* and not simply to facilitate, to act charismatically by taking over ego and superego functions for the group or a specific member. The dependency culture of the inpatient unit creates an atmosphere in which those in positions of authority are readily perceived as being endowed with special healing powers.[11,12] That myth of the dependency culture when used judiciously can bring safety and security to a troubled patient or group.

REFERENCES

1. L. C. Wynne, "Therapies with Schizophrenics," in *Psychotherapy of Schizophrenia*, edited by J. G. Gunderson and L. R. Mosher (New York: Jason Aronson, 1975), pp. 281–292.

2. J. Frosch, *The Psychotic Process* (New York: International Univ. Press, 1983).

3. M. Mendelson, *Psychoanalytic Concepts of Depression* (New York: Spectrum Publications, 1974), pp. 275–287.

---

‡ See Chapter 6, p. 107 for a more complete illustration of this example.

4. G. Adler, *Borderline Psychopathology and its Treatment* (New York: Jason Aronson, 1985).

5. A. H. Modell, "A Narcissistic Defense Against Affects and the Illusion of Self-Sufficiency," *Int. J. Psychoanal.* 56 (1975): 275–282.

6. H. Kohut, *The Analysis of The Self* (New York: International Universities Press, 1977).

7. R. D. Chessick, *Psychology of the Self and the Treatment of Narcissism* (New York: Jason Aronson, 1985).

8. H. L. Muslin, "Heinz Kohut: Beyond the Pleasure Principle," in *Beyond Freud: A Study of Modern Psychoanalytic Theories*, edited by J. Reppen (Hillsdale, N. J.: The Analytic Press, 1985), pp. 203–230.

9. L. R. Ormont, "Group Resistance and the Therapeutic Contract," *Int. J. Group Psychother.* 18 (1967): 147–154.

10. R. W. Betcher, "The Treatment of Depression in Brief Inpatient Group Psychotherapy," *Int. J. Group Psychother.* 33 (1983): 365–386.

11. R. Almond, *The Healing Community: The Dynamics of the Therapeutic Milieu* (New York: Jason Aronson, 1974).

12. J. S. Rutan and C. A. Rice, "The Charismatic Leader: Asset or Liability?" *Psychother: Theory, Research and Practice* 18 (1981): 487–492.

8

The Community Meeting

The community meeting is the central group in the hospital, and it serves a number of vital functions. We have found it helpful to think of the community meeting as part small town meeting and part family meeting.

It is like a town meeting in that it is concerned with the management of the hospital community, addressing and fulfilling the numerous tasks that enable a community to work. It is like a family meeting in that it addresses the issues, pleasures, and conflicts, both overt and covert, that arise when people live, eat, and sleep under the same roof.

Those aspects of the community meeting, its centrality, dynamics, structure, and leadership, along with the frame of the meeting are the major themes of this chapter.

THE CENTRAL ROLE OF THE COMMUNITY MEETING
IN THE HOSPITAL

The influence of the community meeting on the rest of the community and on other treatments does not happen by magic. It happens because most of the other treatment systems of the hospital are subsystems of the community meeting. The members of the different therapy groups are together at the community meeting, therapists and their individual patients are there, those who give medication and those who receive it are present at the meeting, and so on. In brief, the boundaries between the various treatment subsystems become very open and permeable during community meetings so that the information, emotions, and values of that meeting instantly become part of the other treatments.

The community meeting also facilitates much of the communication within, and general functioning, of the psychiatric hospital or unit. It is the place where staff and patients address the tasks of living and working together, where information about the hospital is disseminated, where complaints are heard and addressed, where new members to the community are introduced and departing members are bid farewell, and so on. It is the place where patients not only listen to what the "hospital" has to say, but also the place where they have an opportunity to participate actively in the community, to influence that community and their own treatment, and where the "hospital" can hear what they have to say.

Although a community meeting is not a therapy group, it should serve therapeutic functions. Patients' behavior in the community meeting reflects who they are. Their assets and liabilities, and their nuclear concerns are reflected in how they talk about and respond to the host of items and events that arise in a meeting, such as sharing a room, or sharing a television set, off-ground privileges, meal changes, conflicts around visitors, cleaning up rooms, personal and community crises. In dealing with these numerous matters the patients have an opportunity to further understand themselves and to learn and try out new ways of behaving and of relating to their peers in a large social unit.

EXAMPLE. *Two roommates, Tonya and Vicky, had kept the staff on edge most of the evening. Throughout the evening Vicky wandered through the unit sleeping in other patients' rooms. When she was found sleeping in one patient's room she was immediately returned to her own room, only to leave again and begin looking for another room in which to sleep. Each time she was returned to her room Tonya would waken and protest furiously about being wakened. These protests usually culminated in angry tirades directed at the staff and Vicky.*

The matter came up for discussion at the next day's community meeting. After some persuasion Vicky began to verbalize her concerns. Tonya, she said, was taking up all the space in her room. For example, Tonya had her dresses hanging across the middle of the room so that Vicky could not get to Tonya's half of the room. Tonya had her traveling cases locked and lying in the middle of the floor and would not let Vicky cross over them. Tonya seemed to have so much, and Vicky felt squeezed out. It took Vicky a long time to tell her story, because she was so frightened and withdrawn. Tonya's response was swift and to the point. She accused Vicky of stealing things from her drawers. "I had to protect myself." Other members of the community also accused Vicky of stealing. Vicky was confused, saying she did not steal. In time, however, incontrovertible evidence was produced showing that Vicky had taken things from a number of patients' rooms. Vicky remained confused, claiming she was not stealing. She liked the things she saw and took them to look at, not to steal them.

With help from the community Vicky was able to talk about feeling that she did not have enough and to learn that others knew what it was like to not have enough. The others helped her learn that it was all right to like things and want to see them, but that it was better to ask to see them than to take them.

Covert values also have a profound effect on the community. Those values are often difficult to address, yet their influence is so strong that they can easily undermine the effectiveness of the overt values of the meeting.

EXAMPLE.* *A new therapist was assigned to lead the community meeting. He was very enthusiastic about the role, and he was an active leader. However, his impact on the meeting and afterward on the patients and staff was troublesome. Patients became unusually belligerent in their groups and complained incessantly about the community meeting. Staff also complained and began to miss community meetings. Over time matters got worse rather than better.*

Careful examination of this leader's style indicated that despite his enthusiasm and willingness to lead he did not value either the staff or the patients. When patients raised issues in the meeting he interpreted most of what they said as expressions of their "pathology", thus devaluing them. He often subtly criticized comments made by the staff. All of this devaluing took place outside of his awareness. Consciously, he valued patients and staff alike. The impact of these covert values can usually be rectified once they are brought into awareness and modified. In this instance, it required changing the community meeting leadership.

Although our illustration discusses one person, it is clearly possible for covert values to be shared by more than one person and have even more devastating effects.

THE DYNAMICS OF THE COMMUNITY MEETING

The community meeting shares the dependency group culture of the hospital and of the therapy groups.† Like therapy groups it also

---

* This case example can be found in more detail in Chapter 4, pp. 76–77.
† See Chapter 3.

exhibits numbers of the other developmental phases and is highly inter-actional in nature. In contrast with therapy groups, the community meet-ing tends to be much less stable, with a far greater tendency to break down into subgroups. But, when well organized it can fulfill tasks and influence the community in ways that are not possible in a therapy group.

DEPENDENCY GROUP FEATURES

A number of factors contribute to the predominance of the depend-ency culture in the community meeting. One of these is clearly that of isomorphism. The culture of the hospital is reflected in all its subsystems, of which the community meeting is one.‡ However, the community meeting itself has at least three additional features that facilitate the establishment of a dependency group culture.

1. The community meeting is another treatment mode within the hospital. It is part of the hospital's care giving role. The com-munity meeting exists to facilitate patient's healing and the heal-ing capacities of the hospital and all the other treatment modes. Caretaking is conducive to dependency.
2. The role of authority is very important in the community meet-ing. Patients look to staff, who are their caretakers elsewhere in the hospital, for help in participating in the meetings, and staff along with the patients look to the leader or leaders to provide direction and organization of the meeting. This is true even in those instances where patients lead the meeting. The effective-ness of patient leadership is very dependent on the support of the staff as well as on the patient's skills.
3. Like other groups within the hospital, the community meeting is constantly forming and reforming as patients and staff join and leave the community. That is, the community meeting is forever beginning.

One of the primary benefits of the dependency culture is univer-sality: the recognition that one is not alone. The universality experienced in the community meeting differs in emphasis from that in therapy groups, focusing more on the shared experiences of living in the hospital and less on shared symptoms. In the community meeting patients learn

---

‡ See Chapters 2 and 5 for a more detailed discussion of this issue.

that others have discomforts about being in the hospital, dealing with medication, sharing a room, hospital food, the behavior or misbehavior of some patients, the neglect of staff, schedules, and the many other exigencies of living in a community. They also share the pleasures of living in a community. They experience and hear how members help each other, how others have gotten well and returned to their families and their jobs, how staff have been helpful, how groups have helped, the value of medication, and so on. The members model their behavior after staff, learn how to relate to their peers, and carry some limited responsibilities within the community.

Community meetings also experience other developmental phases, often within one session. There are times when the meeting appears to be in disarray as members protest the conditions of their treatment or passively resist participation. At other times the community may seem strikingly mature as numbers of members say good-bye and encourage their peers to work on their problems so that they too can leave. All these processes and developmental phases are generated by the interactions among the members.

ADDITIONAL DYNAMICS OF COMMUNITY MEETINGS

There are, however, ways in which the dynamics of the community meeting differ from those of the small group.

The Essential Instability of the Community Meeting. Community meetings are essentially unstable groups. Part of this instability is created by the rapid turnover of membership. Even in settings where this is not true, such as a hospital for chronic patients, they continue to be unstable. The instability is created by a number of additional factors that are indigenous to all community meetings. First, the resources of the individual members are often such that stable bonding is not readily possible. Some members are so anxious that they can barely remain in a meeting. Second, the large size of the community meeting makes stable bonding more difficult. When bonding does take place it will often take place in small subgroups within the larger group, thus threatening to fragment the whole.

In large unstable groups undergoing rapid change or facing a crisis, members frequently hunger for a messianic or charismatic leader who can bring certainty and order to their lives.[1,2] A charismatic leader can be very beneficial, as in India under Ghandi, and can be for a hospital community as Almond[3] has demonstrated. But there are grave dangers as well, reflected in such social and national catastrophes as Jones Town and Nazi Germany. Redl[4] describes a similar phenomenon when he discusses the central figures around which groups form. Some brought organization, stability, and affectionate bonding to the group, whereas others brought stability at the cost of distrust and sadistic behavior among the members, particularly toward those who might threaten the groups' stability. The central figures most likely to induce such behavior he described as tyrannical.

In summary, because of the community meeting's inherent instability, its members are susceptible to the vagaries of charismatic and "strong" leadership that may be helpful or seriously detrimental. Furthermore, therapists who lead community meetings are subject to the charismatic hunger of the members and respond to it in ways that are consistent with their own intrapsychic structures. For example, therapists who are prone to sadistic responses when under pressure are likely to create order in the meeting through punitive means and thus increase the danger of the meeting for its members. Others who are able to tolerate the charismatic demands without either trying to fulfill them or deny them can use their role more effectively to provide adequate structure and safety. Clearly, to effectively lead a community meeting it is important that therapists have an understanding of the dynamics of the meetings and of themselves.

Subgrouping in the Community Meeting. All groups, large or small, are subject to breaking into small subgroups. Larger, unstable groups, such as a community meeting, are particularly prone to that breakdown. In a commuity meeting the subgroups often form around central figures who are perceived as more charismatic than the leader of the meeting. Breakdowns of this nature can ultimately cripple the community meeting and make it extrememly difficult for the staff to manage.

A breakdown in the social fabric of the community meeting often leads to a parallel psychological breakdown in the members themselves. Patients may become increasingly psychotic, excessively withdrawn, overwhelmingly agitated, or unruly and leave or be asked to leave the meeting.

Those same dynamics, however, when understood can be turned to productive use.

The Systemic Dynamics of the Community Meeting. Entropy refers to the tendency of all living systems to gravitate toward disorganization and disintegration. Community meetings are a particularly vivid illustration of that process. Living systems counteract that trend, and move toward better organization and greater and more sophisticated integration to the extent that they are able to continually reorganize and restructure themselves. Firm and clear organization and structure are essential if large groups are to function effectively.

When well-structured, large groups can carry out numerous important tasks and produce goods that smaller groups are incapable of doing. A sound structure counteracts the tendency toward entropy. The large group's proclivity to subgroup, for example, can be used as a vehicle for the delegation of responsibility, which increases the organization's capacity to carry out numerous tasks at the same time. Saravay in describing this capacity of the large group wrote:

> Membership in larger organizations is accomplished with a minimum of transitory regression, . . . the established functions and role differentiation within an organization, the aims, rules and regulations defined by and represented in the position of the formal leader, all inhibit the initial regression induced in new members and may assist them . . . to achieve a level of functioning surpassing their experience outside the organization.[5]

THE FRAME OF THE COMMUNITY MEETING

The organization of the community meeting is often referred to as the frame. Several factors in the frame deserve special attention.

THE PLACE

A room that is large enough to seat the whole community with reasonable comfort should be set aside for the meeting. The same room should be used for all meetings. This provides a clear and constant physical framework and helps to increase the stability of the meeting.

THE SEATING ARRANGEMENT

A variety of seating arrangements can be used in community meetings. One method is to have the members sit in a circle, much as in a therapy group. This allows the members to have eye contact with each other and with the leaders. They can also talk directly to one another. It works most effectively in a small community. But in a large circle it often is very difficult to see other people on the same side as oneself, not to mention the fact that few rooms will hold 50 or more people in a circle.

Another seating arrangement common in a larger community is the classroom or row style, where members sit in rows of chairs, armchairs, or couches. It provides some organization and structure in a large community and facilitates getting on with the business of the meeting. The disadvantages are that it is difficult to see all participants, and many members can be a long way from the leadership and from the action. It is more difficult to manage the meeting and listen to the input from the members when not everyone can be seen by the leaders.

Between these two lie a variety of other arrangements, some of which are a modification of the circular style, and some of the classroom style. Those variations are usually determined by the unique structures and shapes of the meeting room.

A form that we have found to be very valuable with a large meeting is semicircular seating. The semicircle usually reduces the number of rows in the meeting, and keeps most members within view of the leaders and helps maintain lively interaction among the members.

Whichever seating method is chosen, the purpose is to encourage as much interaction as possible and to permit the participants to be as readily seen by the leaders and by each other as circumstances will allow. It is important that a viable seating arrangement be determined and then used regularly.

To facilitate the management of the meeting and to prevent unnecessary regression, staff should be evenly dispersed throughout the room. It can be helpful to have additional staff seated near patients who are particularly anxious or who may be especially troublesome. The additional staff in those areas can provide support for the anxious patients and help contain those prone to disruptive behavior.

THE GROUND RULES

Like therapy groups, community meetings should have clear "outside" and "inside" contracts or ground rules.§ Leaders of community

---

§ For a fuller discussion of these contracts see Chapters 5 and 6.

meetings should negotiate with the adminstration conditions that support the optimal running and maintenance of the community meeting. The frame, including the following ground rules, should be agreed on with the administration before a community meeting is established. The ground rules of the community meeting are similar to those of the therapy group.

1. All available staff and patients agree to attend each meeting and stay for the entire session. The availability of patients is, of course, dependent on their condition. Recently admitted patients, for example, may be too distraught to deal with the demands of a community meeting and may have to wait several days before attending. The availability of staff will be affected by the shift on which they work, on emergency requirements, and so on. Otherwise all available patients and staff agree to attend.

This agreement helps to provide constancy and stability in the community meeting. In addition, it places the issues of trust and responsibility at the center of the community's life, because how staff and patients respond to and maintain this agreement has a significant effect on the safety and viability of the community. Frequent absences by staff and/or patients can readily undermine the trust members have for each other.

Included in this agreement is the understanding that no other treatments, with the exception of emergencies and the care of patients whose condition does not permit them to attend, should take place during community meetings. Providing other treatment during these meetings makes it impossible for the patients and the staff involved to fulfill their agreement to the community and, as described above, undermines the trust among the members.

2. Staff and patients agree to communicate by talking. This agreement is important in a meeting of any community. It is an agreement that is understood, if not stated, in most public meetings whether they are town meetings or election debates. It is perhaps especially important in a community meeting because some of the members have considerable difficulty with impulse control and thus often act rather than talk.

The emphasis on speaking rather than acting contains within it the agreement to communicate honestly, especially about issues related to living in the hospital community and to do so in a manner that acknowledges the right of others to speak as well.

THE STRUCTURE AND LEADERSHIP
OF THE COMMUNITY MEETING

There are many ways to structure and lead a community meeting. The methods chosen by a particular hospital are determined by the orientation of the hospital, its size, the style of leadership, the nature of its patient population, and so on. The suggestions that we are about to make refer to a relatively short-term unit with a psychodynamic orientation. Much of what is discussed, however, is also applicable to state hospitals and other longer term facilities.

The question these suggestions seek to answer is: given our understanding of individuals in severe emotional distress and the dynamics of community meetings, what are the essential ingredients to running the meeting effectively?

THE STRUCTURE OF THE MEETING

In addition to establishing clear ground rules, a degree of formal structure is essential in leading an effective community meeting. First, this enables the meeting to work effectively and its members to function more constructively than they would otherwise. Second, it enables the members to deal with tasks necessary for the successful management of the community: the "town meeting" attributes of the community meeting. Management tasks include such things as planning off-grounds trips, dividing up community jobs, dealing with messy rooms, the effects of sunbathing on people taking certain psychotropic medication, and where visitors may be met.

Third, an effective structure must also permit the members to address the personal and interpersonal aspects of their relationships as well as management issues: the "family" attributes of the community meeting. These attributes include such things as squabbles among community members, conflicts with staff, success in treatment, missing friends and family, feeling despair, and the repetition of old problems with roommates and others.

In summary, an effective structure must enable the community to deal with both management and affectively laden interpersonal concerns. Failure to address either is detrimental to the community. A meeting that deals only with management concerns leaves important affective concerns to surface in some other part of the hospital in a less manageable form. A meeting that deals only with affective and interpersonal concerns leaves members without clear expectations about their role and behavior in the hospital, and robs them of the opportunity to take some responsibility for the effective running of the community. Members then fall back on misinformation and rumor to manage their relationship to the hospital, which quickly destroys trust among patients and staff and makes effective management of the community very difficult.

In practice, then, it is helpful to allow adequate time for all members to be recognized and new members introduced and welcomed, to make announcements about community events, discuss items from previous meetings that were to be acted on by the staff, patients, or others. Ample time should also be allowed for discussion of the immediate concerns of the members, and where applicable, opportunity should be given to understand and resolve conflicts. Lastly, some time should be left to say good-bye to patients and staff who are leaving.

These items cannot all be given equal weight. On some occasions important announcements regarding hospital events may take precedence because of the impact those events will have on the life of the hospital community. At other times current concerns of patients may take precedence, and at others saying good-bye to patients who are leaving. Clearly, the structure needs to accommodate the primary adaptive tasks of the community. However, allowing for that necessary flexibility, it is important that leaders have a clear direction when leading a community meeting. Asking, in the midst of a well-structured meeting, "What's on people's minds?" may be a helpful way to encourage discussion about current concerns. But as a frame for beginning a meeting bereft of other structure it can lead to unnecessary regression among the members.

The following is an example of how a community meeting may be structured.

General Welcome and Statement of the Purpose of the Meeting. This is usually a very brief statement indicating the beginning of the meeting. The following is an example of an opening statement. "Welcome to Unit X's community meeting. This is where we talk about living in the hospital together. We talk about the things we like and dislike about living in this community and how we may change some of those things and live with those that we cannot change. It is here that we welcome new members to our community and say good-bye to those who are leaving." Patients who have been at the hospital for some time may be asked to describe the purpose of the meeting, thus increasing the amount of responsibility patients take in the meeting.

Introductions. All members introduce themselves by name, and those who are new are noted and welcomed to the hospital. This introduction recognizes everyone, particularly new members who can begin to make some initial contact in this relatively safe manner. Sometimes new members meet their prospective roommates at the community meeting thus allowing the initial ''hellos'' to be said in a safe environment. Occasionally, an ''old'' member may not want a new roommate and will say so. Disconcerting as that may be, it should be forthrightly addressed and discussed in the meeting, and the reason for not wanting a roommate understood. The injury to the new member can also be addressed and a process of healing begun.

This introduction gives all patients and staff a chance to participate, even if only very briefly, and allows the leaders to learn the names of the participants. Whenever possible leaders should address members by their names.

Announcements. At this juncture the leaders pass onto specific information about events or plans that will affect the community. This may include things such as schedule changes, fire drills, staff vacations, parties, committees to be formed, and movie schedules.

Review Issues of the Previous Meeting. A review of the previous meeting can be done in a variety of ways. The leaders may simply list a number of items that were to be looked into between meetings, or may ask the members of the community to let them know what items or requests were to be followed up on. Some community meetings have patients volunteer to take minutes of each meeting. At this point in the meeting the minutes of the previous meeting would be read and unfinished business addressed.

There are a variety of ways by which leaders can see that relevant business from previous meetings is addressed. The approaches are only limited by staff and patient creativity and the ground rules of the meeting. What is important is that it is done because of its importance to the community.

Discussing business from previous meetings rewards the community members attempts to address ''those things that can be changed'' and assures them that they have been heard. It is not uncommon for a great deal of time to be spent in community meetings dealing with patient complaints. Often simply having the opportunity to complain is adequate, particularly with regard to matters that cannot be changed. But there are matters that can and should be changed, and there are requests that can legitimately be met. From the review of previous meetings patients learn what has happened to their requests and what steps have been taken to bring about agreed on changes. When requests are answered and changes made the patients feel empowered. In addition, the review provides continuity between meetings.

General Guided Discussion.   This discussion usually comprises the bulk of the meeting, and is normally a discussion of current community concerns. Sometimes these concerns arise during the meeting itself, but often they are simply a continuation of issues that first arose in some other part of the hospital. The discussion may center around almost any conceivable issue. This portion of the meeting demands the greatest skill from the leaders in that they must maintain enough structure to allow for reasonable, if at times, heated discussions, on the one hand, and permit enough freedom to allow the members to participate as freely as possible on the other.

Ending the Meeting.   The ending of the meeting is designed to allow for a brief wrap up of the discussion followed by farewells to those who are leaving. The length of the ending period, like other portions of the meeting varies from session to session. Whatever the actual length of the ending phase, however, it should be long enough to allow those who are leaving and those who are left behind to say good-bye as well as they are able. Clearly, when more people are leaving a greater amount of time should be allowed. It is critically important that the meetings end on time. This point will be elaborated below.

Finally, at the close of the meeting it is helpful to remind members of the time of the next meeting.

The Leadership of the Meeting

Leading a community meeting can be an exciting and demanding task. Like the chairperson of a board, leaders must organize and address the agenda of the meeting in an orderly fashion, and like the orchestra conductor must draw forth ''music'' from the individual players and from the orchestra-as-a-whole. In the words of our earlier metaphor, they must address both ''town meeting'' or management issues and ''family'' or affective and interpersonal issues.

Ground Rules and Structure for Leading. It is the role of community meeting leaders to maintain the ground rules and the structure of the meeting.

Maintaining the ground rules requires support from staff. This is particularly true with regard to beginning on time. To begin on time, the room has to be prepared in advance, and patients reminded ahead of time. Preparing the room may mean little more than being sure that it is available at community meeting time. But in some settings it may mean tidying the room, rearraging the seating, and asking visitors to leave. It is helpful if the leaders can gain the cooperation and help of staff members to see that this is done in time. Patients can also help with this preparation.

Staff assistance is also required to remind patients when the community meeting is about to begin. This includes public announcements in halls and main living and dining areas in addition to visits to patients' sleeping quarters.

Once the preliminary work has been done, it is important that the meeting begin on time and that the staff as well as the patients be present at the start of the meeting.

It is also important that the meeting end at the agreed time. Maintaining the time frame reinforces the community meeting boundaries and increases its safety. Unnecessary shortening or lengthening of the meeting reduces its safety. When the time frame of a group has been set the members unconsciously gear themselves to that frame[6] and will introduce material accordingly. This leads to the characteristic beginning, middle, and end phases of a group. Sometimes patients introduce important material near the end of the meeting precisely because it is near the end. By doing so they can introduce the material and postpone discussion of it until a later time when they can better handle it. It is better to acknowledge the importance of the material introduced and place it on the agenda for the next meeting than to prolong the meeting. Where appropriate it can be helpful to suggest that the matter be discussed in group and individual therapy as well.

Once the meeting is underway the leaders should encourage as much participation by the members as possible and see that all who wish to participate have a fair opportunity to do so. In practice this means inviting comments from the members and acknowledging and rewarding any communications they make.

> EXAMPLE. *Todd, a tall, blond young man, stood up in the middle of a community meeting in response to the leaders' request for comments regarding some unrest on the unit. He said he had a poem he wished to recite. He paced back and forth several times in an ungainly and highly nervous manner. The meeting became very tense and the leaders began to regret their request.*
>
> *He began by wishing peace to all. His language then became highly-idiosyncratic and the poem was very hard to follow. The leaders wondered how much time they should allow him. One of them asked Todd how much more time he needed. Todd responded very clearly, saying, "not much longer." A few minutes later Todd stopped by expressing his fear of war, and sat down. The meeting was still tense, as much in response to Todd's anxiety as to his unusual speech.*
>
> *One of the leaders thanked Todd for his poem and said he knew that conflict could be very frightening, but hoped that this community could be as peaceful as Todd wished. In this instance the leader was able to discern a deeper meaning to what on the surface appeared to be a nonsensical communication.*

Making sure that all members have a fair opportunity to participate may, on occasion, mean intervening firmly and respectfully when a patient or staff member prevents others from finishing their comments or from making any at all.

> EXAMPLE. *Wendy had caused a great deal of trouble on the floor the evening before. She had been caught in the middle of several water fights and some staff suspected that she had masterminded the "escape" of one of the patients who ran away. During the community meeting Tim, a staff member, began to quiz her about her behavior. He wanted to know what she had done and why she had done it. He shared with her the rumors he had heard and wanted to know if they were true. Other members tried to make comments but Tim and Wendy were caught in a dialogue that left little time or space for others. The more Tim pressed the more Wendy resisted and protested.*
>
> *The leader of the meeting said, "This is clearly a very important matter. I think it would be helpful if we could hear from other staff and patients as well as from Tim and Wendy." A lively discussion ensued. Some blamed Wendy and some supported her. But in the end it became clear that Wendy was not alone in creating trouble. Indeed she was a relatively minor player, but she was the kind of player who always gets caught.*

To maintain the structure of the community meeting it is important that the leaders allow adequate time for the discussion of the major agenda items of the meeting as described earlier. This means determining when a piece of business has been dealt with adequately and it is time to move on to the next item, or knowing when an agenda item needs additional time because of its impact on the community.

How to Lead: Listening and Intervening. Listening is one of the primary functions of community meeting leaders, and most of the guidelines for listening in therapy groups apply also.* The primary difference is one of emphasis. The difference in emphasis is created by the goals of the community meeting. Community meetings are primarily concerned with enabling the community to manage itself and the complex personal and interpersonal dynamics that arise when people live together in close quarters.

In community meetings leaders not only listen to the overt content but they address it much more directly than in therapy groups, as with Todd's poem discussed previously. The overt material is frequently related to community management and responding to it often facilitates the smooth running of the community. When members of a community meeting complain about a shortage of food or inadequate seating at dinner tables it is important to address those concerns directly and where applicable and possible to correct the situation. As noted earlier, when suitable corrections are made the members feel empowered and the meeting has effectively performed one of its functions. Similarly, when a conflict arises between two or more members of the community it is important that the members have an opportunity to work out a practical solution to their dilemma.

> EXAMPLE. *Walter and Ted exchanged barbs at the beginning of a community meeting. Ted claimed that Walter had stolen his clothes. The leaders asked them to tell what had happened and this story emerged. Earlier Ted had gone to the laundry room to pick up his clothes from the dryer and found that they were gone. He said he saw Walter carrying his clothes basket up to his room. Walter said adamantly that it was his basket. Further discussion revealed that there were several clothes baskets in the hospital the same color as Walter's and Ted's and there was often a confusion. Roseanne, an occupational therapist, said she had seen a basket of the same color outside the Occupational Therapy room. With help*

---

* See Chapter 6 for a detailed discussion of this matter.

> *from the community Walter and Ted agreed that they would meet with*
> *Roseanne after the meeting and check out the two baskets. Sure enough,*
> *they found Ted's basket outside the Occupational Therapy room.*

Addressing the overt content in this manner not only solved a conflict within the community, but it also demonstrated how differences could be resolved without having to resort to accusations. Similarly, it is important to address directly the many other concerns that arise in community meetings around medication side effects, attendance at groups, changes in menus, fire drills, and so on. Additionally, when patient's concrete day-to-day concerns are openly addressed and attended to they tend to be more receptive to addressing covert issues as well.

When the overt issues have been adequately addressed, leaders should then address the covert concerns of the members. Our earlier account of the conflict between Vicky and Tonya illustrates this process. After a long discussion of Vicky's nighttime wanderings and stealing, and the other events of the previous evening, the community then addressed the covert communications behind Vicky's behavior. They not only asked that she not steal anymore, but more important, acknowledged her loneliness and isolation that had led to the stealing in the first place. They let Vicky know that she was not alone.

Often the covert content of a meeting reflects the concerns of the whole community and not just one or two of the members.

> EXAMPLE. *Trish, a member of the senior staff, complained about the*
> *number of dirty plates and pieces of food that had been left lying around*
> *the common room. She asked that everyone take responsibility for his or*
> *her food and plates and return them to the kitchen when finished. Numbers*
> *of patients agreed with Trish and spoke of how embarrassed they had*
> *been when visitors dropped by to see them. Trish's complaint was followed*
> *by complaints from patients. Joey complained that every time he tried to*
> *watch television it was taken over by a "lot of women" who watched soap*
> *operas. Paula complained that Joey was forever switching channels and*
> *making loud noises. Others complained that while they were trying to*
> *watch television some people were playing loudly on the piano and the*
> *staff had done nothing about it.*
>
> *Each complaint was dealt with in turn and some tacit agreements arrived at. It soon became clear, however, that there was more to these conflicts than met the eye. The tacit agreements did little to settle them, their number seemed endless and they frequently focused around food, the sharing of space, and the inability or unwillingness of the staff to do anything about it.*
>
> *Then one of the leaders realized that a lot of staff had been out ill*

recently. He said to the community, "we have all been under a lot of stress recently. Many of the staff have been out ill. Those of us who have been on the unit have been unable to pay as much attention to you as we usually do. So its not surprising that everyone is feeling upset and angry. Let's talk about it." That clarifying interpretation made sense of the community's experience. Slowly the members began to talk about the staff who were missing, and what it was like when they couldn't find a staff person to talk to. Some staff also spoke about what it was like for them to be short-handed.

Although much is to be gained by addressing the overt and covert issues in a community meeting, there are times when addressing either or both seems to have little impact. Some meetings seem to be nothing more than a litany of complaints, whereas others are depressing and filled with long, heavy silences. During such meetings one is severely tempted to throw in the towel, cut the meetings short, or cancel them altogether and go home.

These low points are part of the ebb and flow of the community's life, a community that has usually had more than its share of life's pain and loss. When a large portion of a recently stable community is discharged it is not uncommon for succeeding community meetings to be heavy and listless, and for others to seem fragmented and disjointed as large numbers of new patients are being added. It is important during these periods to maintain the meetings as always, knowing that in doing so the foundation is being laid for more effective meetings in the future. And more important, patients are provided with a stable environment while they grieve the losses and cope with the changes in their community. If patients are abandoned in the community meeting, they will soon feel abandoned elsewhere, including in their groups. And having been abandoned in the community meeting, it would hardly be surprising if they abandoned the groups and their other treatments in turn.

REFERENCE

1. Z. A. Liff, "The Charismatic Leader," in *The Leader and The Group*, edited by Z. A. Liff (New York: Jason Aronson, 1975), pp. 114–122.

2. J. S. Rutan and C. A. Rice, "The Charismatic Leader: Asset or Liability?" *Psychother.: Theory, Research Pract.* 18 (1981): 487–492.

3. R. Almond, *The Healing Community* (New York: Jason Aronson, 1974).

4. F. Redl, "Group Emotion and Leadership," in *Psychoanalytic Group Dynamics: Basic Readings*, edited by S. Scheidlinger (New York: International Universities Press, 1982), pp. 15–68.

5. S. M. Saravay, ''Group Psychology and the Structural Theory: A Revised Psychoanalytic Model of Group Psychology,'' in *Psychoanalytic Group Dynamics*, edited by S. Scheidlinger (New York: International Universities Press, 1982), pp. 255–275.

6. C. A. Rice, ''Observations on the Unexpected and Simultaneous Termination of Leader and Group,'' *Group* 1 (1977):100–117.

Epilogue

By the crowd they have been broken, by the crowd they can be healed.[1]

There is still the ring of truth to that motto of L. Cody Marsh. Although we have learned much since Marsh's time about the many factors that contribute to mental illness, from the biological to the environmental, it is still true that the relationships in an individual's life, particularly the early primary relationships, play a profound role in determining how that person will grow and mature emotionally, and how he or she will adapt to the biological and social givens in life. Where there is an optimum degree of love and intimacy, autonomy and respect between individuals and their earliest caretakers the likelihood that they will experience healthy emotional growth and maturity is greatly increased. Where love and intimacy, autonomy and respect are missing or distorted, the possibility of emotional growth and maturity is seriously compromised, even with the best biological and environmental givens.

Inpatient group therapy cannot undo the past nor can it provide the optimum family experience many of our patients never had. But it can provide a relatively safe set of relationships in which patients discover that they are not alone, and where they can begin to understand the solutions they have devised to maintain contact with their fellow humans and with themselves. Those solutions usually make sense given their life experiences, but often at the expense of the personal relationships and sense of identity they want and need. Not uncommonly they discourage relationships and occasionally they can be quite destructive. The young woman who slashes her wrist because she wants to feel something and know that she is alive. The man who tries to compensate for feeling inadequate by putting others down, ends up isolating himself from those he needs most. Inpatient groups provide an environment where those

173

repetitive behaviors stand out in bold relief and thus can be understood and slowly begin to change.

We have suggested how those groups can be established and led. We have emphasized the importance of the hospital environment in which the groups are set, and the necessity of working in close conjunction with the rest of the staff. We have underlined the importance of listening to what our patients say, both overtly and covertly, noting that interventions are most effective if they are based on a clear understanding of our patients' communications. To improve our listening we have emphasized the importance of understanding the dynamics of the individual patients, groups, community meetings, and the hospital itself.

However, valuable as the guidelines and suggestions of a book may be, it is no substitute for practice supported by good supervision and self-understanding. Hence, an essential ingredient in any group therapy program is supervision or consultation by professionals who are well versed in the field and skilled in practice. This is often done best in a group of peers led by a senior clinician. When such supervisory groups are well led, they provide therapists with an opportunity to discuss the events in their groups with an immediacy that is not possible through books or lectures. They can describe and analyze the many nuances of an individual session, or the ebb and flow of the group process from session to session. They can examine their own responses to the members' interactions, and learn how understanding those responses can help them to intervene effectively. They also learn by giving and receiving consultation to and from their peers, and by hearing how they lead their groups.

Undergoing personal psychotherapy, particularly in a psychodynamic group, can be an important asset to inpatient group therapists. This is especially true if therapists find themselves experiencing repeated difficulties in working with their groups. The importance of self-understanding for therapists is seen most clearly when we realize that our humanity is our primary therapeutic instrument.

REFERENCE

1. S. B. Hadden, "A Glimpse of Pioneers in Group Psychotherapy," *Int. J. Group Psychother.* XXV (1975): 374.

Index